# South Carolina Ballads

# South Carolina Ballads

WITH A STUDY OF THE

TRADITIONAL BALLAD TO-DAY

Collected and Edited by

REED SMITH

*The Black Heritage Library Collection*

BOOKS FOR LIBRARIES PRESS
FREEPORT, NEW YORK
1972

First Published 1928
Reprinted 1972

Reprinted from a copy in the
Fisk University Library Negro Collection

INTERNATIONAL STANDARD BOOK NUMBER:
0-8369-8991-0


LIBRARY OF CONGRESS CATALOG CARD NUMBER:
74-38025


PRINTED IN THE UNITED STATES OF AMERICA
BY
NEW WORLD BOOK MANUFACTURING CO., INC.
HALLANDALE, FLORIDA 33009

TO

GEORGE LYMAN KITTREDGE

# PREFACE

THIS little book is the result of almost a score of years of browsing in the fascinating field of traditional balladry. On the side of theory, it starts with the popular ballad as we have it exhibited in Child's great collection, and works forward in time to modern instances and contemporary analogies, with all possible stress on music as an essential part of ballads. What is said of communal composition makes for itself only one claim: it is written with malice toward none, and is at least good-natured.

The second part contains a small sheaf of surviving South Carolina ballads and two traditional songs. The ballads number fourteen in all, with forty-three variants and twelve tunes. They were collected at odd times by the writer and by other interested persons. To these helpers specific acknowledgment is made in the head-notes to the ballads. Special thanks are due to Margaret Dick Smith, who transcribed and edited nearly all of the tunes.

In addition to the ballads printed below, at least four others are authentically reported for South Carolina, but owing to the accidents and disappointments of ballad-collecting they could not be recorded. They are "The Three Crows" (Child, No. 26), "The Cherry-Tree Carol" (Child, No. 54), "The Lass of Roch Royal" (Child, No. 76), and "The Farmer's Curst Wife" (Child, No. 278).

Much of the material of the following pages has been printed in the columns of the *Columbia State* and as a bulletin of the University of South Carolina. It is gathered together and re-shaped here as another small addition to the growing total of American balladry.

REED SMITH

UNIVERSITY OF SOUTH CAROLINA
January 16, 1928

# CONTENTS

## THE TRADITIONAL BALLAD TO–DAY

## SOUTH CAROLINA BALLADS

x CONTENTS

# ABBREVIATIONS

Campbell and Sharp..Olive Dame Campbell and Cecil J. Sharp, *English Folk Songs from the Southern Appalachians*, G. P. Putnam's Sons, 1917.

Cox ...............J. H. Cox, *Folk-Songs of the South*, Harvard University Press, 1925.

Gerould............G. H. Gerould, "The Making of Ballads," *Modern Philology*, vol. xxi, 1923.

Gummere ........Francis B. Gummere, *The Popular Ballad*, Houghton Mifflin Co., 1907.

Hart ..............W. M. Hart, *English Popular Ballads*, Scott, Foresman and Co., 1922.

Henderson .........T. F. Henderson, *The Ballad in Literature*, Cambridge University Press, 1912.

Kittredge ..........H. C. Sargent and G. L. Kittredge, *English and Scottish Popular Ballads*, Houghton Mifflin Co., 1904.

Pound ............Louise Pound, *Poetic Origins and the Ballad*, Macmillan Co., 1921.

Sharp .............Cecil J. Sharp, *One Hundred English Folksongs*, Oliver Ditson Co., 1916.

Smith .............C. Alphonso Smith, "Ballads Surviving in the United States," *Musical Quarterly*, vol. ii, Jan., 1916.

# South Carolina Ballads

# I

## BALLAD AND FOLK-SONG

A BALLAD is a song that tells a story; or, to put it the other way around, a story told in a song." [1] It is a short story in verse, sung instead of told.

Both folk-song and ballad go back to remotest times. The folk-song is the simplest and most enduring form of either music or poetry. From it are derived not only our scales, but the shape of our melodies, the outlines of our musical form, and, indirectly, the art of harmony and cadences.

In folk-song all three of the golden strands of time-rhythm are blended — poetry, music, and dance. In the beginning, as has been said, there was probably no poem that was not sung, no song that was not danced to, and no dance that was not accompanied by a song. [2]

The difference between folk-song and ballad is largely a matter of subjectivity, that is, the extent to which the personal feeling or attitude of the author shines through and colors the material. The folk-song is subjective; the personal feelings of the writer emerge and speak through it. The ballad is objective and impersonal, the author's personality being entirely withdrawn and the story telling itself, as it were, without human instrumentality.

A fine example of the folk-song is the anonymous Scotch poem of the forsaken girl, dating from about 1700:

> O waly, waly, up the bank!
> And waly, waly, down the brae!
> And waly, waly, yon burn-side,
> Where I and my love wont to gae!

[1] The words are those of Professor Kittredge. A longer descriptive definition is the following: "The popular ballad is a poem meant for singing, quite impersonal in manner, narrative in material, probably connected in its origins with the communal dance, but submitted to a process of oral tradition among people who are free from literary influences and fairly homogeneous in character" (Gummere, p. 2).

[2] Franz Böhme, *Geschichte des Tanzes in Deutschland*, i, 13, 229.

I lent my back unto an aik,
  I thought it was a trusty tree;
But first it bow'd and syne it brak,
  Sae my true-love did lichtly me.

A waly, waly, but love be bonny
  A little time, while it is new;
But when 'tis auld, it waxeth cauld,
  And fades awa' like morning dew.

O wherefore should I busk my head?
  Or wherefore should I kame my hair?
For my true-love has me forsook,
  And says he'll never loe me mair.

Martinmas wind, when wilt thou blaw,
  And shake the green leaves aff the tree?
O gentle death, when wilt thou come?
  For of my life I am weary.

'T is not the frost that freezes fell,
  Nor blawing snaw's inclemency;
'T is not sic cauld that makes me cry,
  But my love's heart grown cauld to me.

When we came in by Glasgow town,
  We were a comely sight to see;
My love was clad in the black velvet,
  And I mysell in cramasie.

But had I wist, before I kiss'd,
  That love had been sae ill to win,
I'd lock'd my heart in a case of gold,
  And pin'd it with a silver pin.

Oh, oh, if my young babe were born,
  And set upon the nurse's knee,
And I mysell were dead and gane!
  And the green grass growing over me![1]

Another beautiful folk-song is the anonymous "Lyke-Wake Dirge," which was sung in rural England at funerals early in the seventeenth century. "When any dieth," says an old account

---

[1] From one to four stanzas of this lament have been taken up and incorporated through oral tradition into the ballad of Jamie Douglas, which tells of an alleged similar situation in the Douglas family of Scotland, in 1681. Thus easily do folk-song and ballad intermingle.

of it, "certaine women sing a song to the dead bodie, recyting the journey that the partye deceased must goe." This lament was current during the ballad age, and, like ballads, it has a delicate, yet insistent, pattern of repetition; but, unlike ballads, it is non-narrative in form and is lyric in mood.

### A Lyke-Wake Dirge

This ae night, this ae night,
  Every night and alle;
Fire and sleet, and candle light,
  And Christ receive thy saule.

When thou from hence away art passed,
  Every night and alle;
To Whinny-muir thou comest at last;
  And Christ receive thy saule.

If ever thou gavest hosen and shoon,
  Every night and alle;
Sit thee down and put them on;
  And Christ receive thy saule.

If hosen and shoon thou ne'er gavest nane,
  Every night and alle;
The whinnes shall prick thee to the bare bane;
  And Christ receive thy saule.

From Whinny-muir when thou mayst pass,
  Every night and alle;
To Brig o' Dread thou comest at last;
  And Christ receive thy saule.

If ever thou gavest meat or drink,
  Every night and alle;
The fire shall never make thee shrink;
  And Christ receive thy saule.

If meat or drink thou never gavest nane,
  Every night and alle;
The fire will burn thee to the bare bane;
  And Christ receive thy saule.

This ae night, this ae night,
  Every night and alle;
Fire and sleet, and candle light,
  And Christ receive thy saule.

At the opposite pole from the folk-song, with its individual experience and personal emotion, stands the ballad, with its emphasis on situation and incident, and its entire impersonality of tone.  The author is merely the narrator of events, having no personal connection with them, feeling no personal responsibility for them, seeking only to tell a tragic story, not to lament a tragic fate.[1]

Consider the objectivity of the following familiar ballad passages:

(*Johnnie Cock's mother warns him of the dangers of hunting abroad.*)

> There are seven foresters at Pickeram Side,
>     At Pickeram where they dwell,
> And for a drop of thy heart's bluid
>     They wad ride the fords of hell.

(*Johnnie Armstrong rallies his men in a losing fight.*)

> Saying, "Fight on, my merry men all,
>     I am a little hurt, but I am not slain;
> I will lay me down for to bleed a while,
>     Then I 'l rise and fight with you again."

(*Sir Patrick Spens and his men are drowned on the winter passage from Norway to Scotland.*)

> O lang, lang may their ladies sit,
>     Wi thair fans into their hand,
> Or eir they se Sir Patrick Spence
>     Cum sailing to the land.

> O lang, lang may their ladies stand,
>     Wi thair gold kems in thair hair,
> Waiting for thair ain deir lords,
>     For they 'll se thame na mair.

> Haf owre, haf owre to Aberdour,
>     It 's fiftie fadom deep,
> And thair lies guid Sir Patrick Spence,
>     Wi' the Scot lords at his feit.

---

[1] Not infrequently, however, the ballad refrain furnishes an emotional comment or suggests the emotional background.

The difference between the objectivity of these ballad snatches and the lyric cry of the folk-song is essential. The feeling in the ballads is as intense as it is in the songs, but in the song we weep because the singer is sad; in the ballad we weep because the story is tragic.

The ballad is a popular, not a learned, type. Its birth was on the lips and heart of the people as a whole. Artistic literature, on the other hand, as contrasted with popular literature, received its chief impetus from university, court, and religious circles. The literary types in favor in England both before and after Chaucer's death, like the metrical romance and the lay, were composed by cultured poets for educated people — what are loosely called the upper classes. Literature was aristocratic, because its audience and the patrons for whom it was composed and by whom it was supported belonged to sophisticated circles. Not so with the ballad. It had no concern with patrons or patronage. Like other forms of folk-lore, it was kept alive by oral tradition, not by manuscript. Ballads were composed by the hundreds and sung in the homes of the plain people; they were whistled along the highroads and by-paths of England and Scotland; they were recited in the inns and taverns, in town and country, passing from mouth to mouth and from generation to generation. Only by accident did they gain the permanence of manuscript. For their very self-preservation, therefore, ballads were dependent upon popularity alone. They were popular in the truest sense: they were of the people, by the people, and for the people.

The ballad presents life in its simplest terms. There is no elaboration, reflection, or sophistication. The story is unfolded abruptly, swiftly, and concretely, in broad, simple strokes. It is the lowest common denominator of narrative art. Thus revealing, as it does, not a personality but a universality, the ballad style does not suffer by translation.

As to form, the ballad measure is likewise the easiest and most rapid of English stanza forms, the accents usually being four, three, four, three, on an iambic pattern, with the second and fourth lines rhyming. The language, too, is as simple as possible. There is some accidental alliteration, and the figures of speech are few, mainly metaphors. There is practically no description. Dialogue is frequently and vividly employed. There is much repetition of epithet, phrase, and line, and frequent use of refrain.

The ballad possesses an impersonal power and a direct simplicity lacking in other poetry. It is rude, vigorous, often grim. There is little softening or shading. Its chief themes deal with tragedy pointed with suffering, especially the tragic side of love. Favorite subjects are the episodes of war, lawlessness, poaching, fighting, ambushes, superstition, and enchantment. There are frequent touches of rough humor, and usually gentleness toward women, justice for the oppressed, and mercy for the poor and needy. Sidney Lanier has finely expressed the spirit that breathes through the ballad: "I know that he who walks in the way that these ballads point will be manful in necessary fight, fair in trade, loyal in love, generous to the poor, tender in the household, prudent in living, plain in speech, merry upon occasion, simple in behavior and honest in all things."

Ballads ring true because they are the poetry of a race, and not the unrepresentative work of one man. They come face to face with life and deal unflinchingly with it, as if the heart of the people spoke aloud. We feel their poignancy, tragedy, and noble simplicity. Beside them most other poetry seems artificial and pale.

This is not saying that the ballads are always, or even usually, noble poetry. As a wise ballad-lover has well said: "The great poems of the world are far greater than the greatest ballads; but no poet has ever had the power to compete with popular tradition on its own ground. Art can create far beyond the beauty of sea-shells, and on occasion can exactly reproduce them; but it cannot fashion or imitate their murmur of the sea." [1]

So characteristic of their age were the ballad code and the ballad sanctions, that Andrew Fletcher of Saltoun, Dryden's

[1] Gummere, p. 321.

contemporary, said: "I know a very wise man that believed that
. . . if a man were permitted to make all the ballads, he need not
care who should make the laws of a nation." And Addison, who
neither by temperament, training, nor the time spirit of his age,
was predisposed toward the ballad as a type, wrote in *The
Spectator:* "It is impossible that anything should be universally
tested and approved by a multitude, though they are the rabble
of a nation, which hath not in it some peculiar aptness to please
and gratify the mind of man."

Of recent tributes, that of Andrew Lang has become almost a
classic:[1] "Ballads sprang from the very heart of the people, and
flit from age to age, from lip to lip of shepherds, peasants, nurses,
of all the class that continues nearest to the state of natural men.
They make music with the plash of the fisherman's oars and the
hum of the spinning-wheel, and keep time with the step of the
ploughman as he drives his team. The country seems to have
aided man in their making; the bird's note rings in them, the
tree has lent her whispers, the stream its murmur, the village-
bell its tinkling tune. The whole soul of the peasant class
breathes in their burdens, as the great sea resounds in the shells
cast up on the shores. Ballads are voices from secret places,
from silent peoples and old times long dead; and as such they
stir us in a strangely intimate fashion to which artistic verse can
never attain."

[1] "Ballads," *Encyclopædia Britannica*, ninth ed.

# II

# DRAMATIC, LYRIC, AND
# NARRATIVE TRAITS

ONE of the most interesting things about the ballad is the unique way in which it combines the three chief poetic methods, dramatic, lyric, and epic. In no other poetic form are these three elements so strikingly blended.

The dramatic element is less important than either the lyric or the epic, but it is unmistakably present. Theatrically abrupt beginnings, characters in action and confrontation, conflicting passions brought visibly to bay, vivid action realized through terse dialogue, the rapid tragic catastrophe — all the qualities of the dramatic method occur repeatedly in the ballad. As the poet Gray wrote in 1757 of a version of "Child Maurice": [1] "I have got the old Scotch ballad on which *Douglas* [2] was founded. It is divine . . . Aristotle's best rules are observed in it in a manner which shows that the author had never heard of Aristotle. It begins in the fifth act of the play. You may read it two-thirds through without guessing what it is about; and yet, when you come to the end, it is impossible not to understand the whole story."

With the omission of a few strictly narrative stanzas and the addition of stage directions and *dramatis personae*, many of the ballads could be turned into little plays that would almost act themselves. The action of "Lord Randal," for instance, is entirely carried on in a dialogue between a mother and her son, who is dying of poison administered by his false truelove, each speaking in turn two lines of each stanza. "The Maid Freed from the Gallows," or "The Hangman's Tree," is an even better example. It not only is essentially dramatic,[3] but also illustrates

---

[1] Letter to William Mason.     [2] A play by John Home, first acted in 1756.
[3] See below, pp. 88–89, for instances of this ballad's being converted into a little drama acted out instead of sung.

how readily a song-poem of this type could be learned and sung
in chorus by a group that had never heard it before.

Important, however, as the dramatic element in ballads is,
the lyric element is more important still.  The term "lyric" as applied to poetry has two entirely different yet essential meanings,
and confusion often results from not keeping them distinct.  In
the first sense, lyric means poetry composed for musical accom-
paniment, poetry intended to be sung, or, simply, song-poetry.
In this sense the words of all religious and secular songs are
lyric, as "Lead, Kindly Light," "My Rosary," "Home, Sweet
Home," and "Dixie."  Lyric also are librettos, the texts of light
and grand opera.

In this sense of song-poetry the ballads are, of course essentially lyric.  As songs they began, as songs they live, and as songs
they die.

The fact that ballads are song-poems, not reading-poems, is
all-important.  We children of a later age have come upon the
ballads fixed on the printed page, like butterflies on cardboard.
We sit down in a library and read them silently out of a book,
as we might the poems of Wordsworth or Whitman.  Nothing
could ensure our getting a more partial impression of the actual
thing itself.  Ballads were made to be sung, and should be rel-
ished as songs, not as poems.  Think of the difference between
reading in print the words of "Annie Laurie" and of "Old
Black Joe," and then hearing a singer sing them, or better still,
joining in the chorus ourselves.  Or think of "Abide With Me,"
or "Lead, Kindly Light," first as read from the hymn-book, and
then as sung by choir and congregation.  Or think of the Negro
spirituals, with their often inadequate words, and then of the
rich melody and haunting rhythm of "Swing Low, Sweet
Chariot," "Go Down, Moses," and "Could n't Hear Nobody
Prayin'," as rendered by a group of Negroes.

In the same way, ballads lose their identity when they are
read instead of sung.  The ballad poem is only half the ballad;
the ballad melody is the other half.  It happens, fortunately,
that the words alone, of many of the ballads, constitute real

poetry, and are worth while as poetry read from the printed page. Such are "Sir Patrick Spens," "Bonny James Campbell," "The Hunting of the Cheviot," "Johnnie Cock," "The Twa Brothers," "Edward," "Johnnie Armstrong," "Mary Hamilton," "Jock o' the Side," "The Twa Sisters," "The Wife of Usher's Well," "The Three Ravens," and "Young Waters." But many other ballads, like "The Hangman's Tree," "Lord Randal," and "Barbara Allen," must have their music, or they make little appeal.

Not only so. It is the music that fixes the emotional effect and tone of a ballad. The words of "Lord Lovel," for example, are sad enough: Lord Lovel leaves Lady Ouncebell (or Nancybell) and overstays his time. She pines away and dies. He, too, on his return, sinks under his remorse and grief. The ballad ends:

> Lady Ouncebell died on the yesterday,
>   Lord Lovill on the morrow;
> Lady Ouncebell died for pure true love,
>   Lord Lovill died for sorrow.
>
> Lady Ouncebell was buried in the high chancel,
>   Lord Lovill in the choir;
> Lady Ouncebell's breast sprung out a sweet rose,
>   Lord Lovill's a bunch of sweet briar.
>
> They grew till they grew to the top of the church,
>   And then they could grow no higher;
> They grew till they grew to a true-lover's knot,
>   And then they tyed both together.

This ballad poem is a tragedy. The ballad tune, however, is a lilting air, with triple repetition of the last word, which it is impossible to sing without feeling light-hearted and gay. There is a smile in it all the way. Thus the difference between reading "Lord Lovel" as a poem and singing it as a song is the difference between shadow and sunshine, or tears and laughter. On the other hand, the melodies of "Barbara Allen," "The Hangman's Tree," and most of the ballads are in emotional accord with the action, and greatly enhance the effect of the ballad poems.

The chief thing, therefore, is never to forget that ballads were songs, actually and widely sung by the people and handed down by oral tradition, and that only long after the creative ballad age had passed were they written down, and thus attained the cold permanence of ink.  The only way to get an idea of what they were really like is to play and sing them from a collection containing both words and music.[1]  The mother of James Hogg, the "Ettrick Shepherd," was right when, after singing many folk-songs and ballads for Walter Scott to take down, she said despairingly, "They were made for singing, and no for reading; but ye hae broken the charm now, an they'll never be sung mair."

Thus far, then, concerning lyric in its original sense of song-poetry.  The second and derived meaning of lyric is "subjective": that is, poetry whose purpose is to express the mood and emotion of the poet.  From this angle, the essence of a lyric poem is not what happens, but the poet's reaction to what happens; not what the poet sees, but the way he feels about it.  Thus, what really matters in "Crossing the Bar" is not death but the poet's attitude toward it; in "The Raven," it is not the bird but the lover's grief for his sweetheart; and in "On First Looking into Chapman's Homer," not the greatness of Homer but the delight of Keats.  In all the great elegies — "Astrophel," "Lycidas," "Adonaïs," "Thyrsis," "In Memoriam" — we grieve, not for the dead poet, but with the living one.  Song, sonnet, ode, elegy, the chief lyric types, are lenses through which we look into the poet's heart.  To twist a popular saying, the "I" of the lyric is the window to the soul.

Now, in this sense of being subjective, the ballad is not lyric at all.  It is just the opposite.  It tells a story for the sake of the story, and is thus altogether epic or narrative.  So far from

[1] For instance, C. J. Sharp, *One Hundred English Folksongs*, Oliver Ditson, 1916; O. D. Campbell and C. J. Sharp, *English Folk Songs from the Southern Appalachians*, G. P. Putnam's Sons, 1917; Loraine Wyman and Howard Brockway, *Lonesome Tunes*, H. W. Gray Co., 1916; J. H. Cox, *Folk-Songs of the South*, Harvard University Press, 1925; C. Alphonso Smith, "Ballads Surviving in the United States," *Musical Quarterly*, January, 1916, pp. 109–129; G. L. Kittredge, "Ballads and Songs," *Journal of American Folk-Lore*, vol. xxx, no. 117; Carl Sandburg, *The American Songbag*, Harcourt, Brace & Co., 1927; files of *Journal of American Folk-Lore*.

mirroring the poet's feeling in any way, the ballad is entirely impersonal and not in the least self-revealing. There is no discoverable author, no person, no personality behind it.

Poetry in general is just the reverse. A poem is the characteristic creation of a poet who alone among men could have written it just that way. As the French first said, art is nature seen through a personality. What gives art its value is the strength, truth, and beauty it draws from the heart and soul of the artist. We choose our poets as we do our friends — because they are just themselves and nobody else. If we like Browning better than Tennyson, we do so because we like the characteristic Browning note better than the characteristic Tennyson note. If we prefer Masefield to Masters, it is just because he is John and not Edgar Lee. It is the poet's own personality that lives in his poetry.

The ballad, on the other hand, has no known author. It is an astonishing fact, but true, that we do not know the name of the author of even a single one of the 305 traditional ballads that have come down to us. And this anonymity is not simply a surface matter of absence of signature. It goes deeper. It is organic and fundamental. Should an unsigned poem of Milton or Browning or Poe come to light, we could probably guess its authorship, or at least feel sure that it was written under the influence of, or in imitation of, one or the other. But ballads show no individuality whatever. The story tells itself; the song sings itself.

Author and singer both seem to play merely the rôle of impersonal transmission.

# III

# COMMUNAL COMPOSITION

## I. In Theory

BALLAD origins are uncertain. Several conflicting theories have been advanced to account for such striking ballad characteristics [1] as their freshness, spontaneity, naturalness, unconventionality, impersonality; and their wide use of repetition in its various forms, such as refrain, burden, or chorus, simple repetition of words and phrases, incremental repetition, whereby the same words are repeated in a set of stanzas with just enough change or addition to advance the story one step,[2] recurrence of set epithets, alliterative phrases, and poetic formulas, all of which characteristics are found not only in the ballads of England and of Scotland but in those of Greece, France, Provence, Portugal, Denmark, and Italy as well.

One view is that ballads are the detritus of an older epic oral literature; another is that they were composed by the special minstrel class which existed in England for approximately five hundred years after the Norman Conquest; others think them descended from the dance-songs of primitive peoples; many consider them to have been communally improvised by mediaeval peasant and village throngs; some attribute them to the

---

[1] The marks of folk-poetry as listed by Ampère in France and Lang in England are these: assonance for rhyme; a brusque style of recital; textual repetition; use of dialogue and speeches; fondness for certain numbers like three and seven; lavish use of gold and silver in the commonest objects of everyday life; talking birds; plots and situations common to many countries; non-Christian attitude toward death and the other world; the supernatural and superstitions, transformation by enchantment, return of the dead, elves, fairies, recurring epithets, use of favorite endings or motifs, such as the bush and briar, or two rose-trees, which meet and plait over the graves of unhappy lovers. See "Ballads," *Encyclopædia Britannica*, ninth ed.

[2] As, for example, in "Lord Randal," "The Hangman's Tree," "Babylon," "Hind Horn," "St. Stephen," "Edward," "The Twa Sisters," "The Cruel Brother," and in the nursery extravaganza, "The House that Jack Built."

mediaeval church, holding that short narrative songs on ecclesiastical and Biblical themes first arose among the clergy, and that the type was later secularized, as happened in the case of the drama.

The most interesting of these theories is communal composition. Those who believe in it do not think that a ballad has any individual author at all. Rather is the ballad the group product of a whole community, or folk, under the sway of a strong common emotional stimulus. In the famous and cryptic words of Grimm, "Das Volk dichtet" [1] — the people compose.

This theory offers a fascinating field for conjecture. It is easy to explain in theory, but hard to prove in fact. It has long been the favorite battleground of ballad enthusiasts both in Europe and in America, and many a good fight has been fought over it. As was remarked of a literary controversy in Queen Elizabeth's day: "Faith, there has been much to-do on both sides, and the nation holds it no sin to tarre them on to controversy. Oh, there has been much throwing about of brains." It has even been suggested that but for their fascinating mystery, the learned world would not have preoccupied itself, in the same measure, with ballads. [2]

Those who hold with communal composition do so with many reservations and modifications. There are as many kinds and degrees of belief in it as there are, say, in evolution. Most authorities agree in considering communal composition possible only in a primitive, or at least a highly naïve and unsophisticated, state of society.

Now the difference between primitive and civilized society is incredibly great. They are literally different worlds. So far as literature is concerned, for example, "poet" to us suggests Vergil spending ten years over the *Aeneid*, Milton and the labor of *Paradise Lost*, Gray and the super-revision of the *Elegy*, and Poe and the self-conscious artistry of "The Raven." But "among

---

[1] As Professor Kittredge points out (Kittredge, p. xviii, n. 1), this phrase is to be regarded as a summing up of Grimm's theory rather than as a direct quotation.

[2] Pound, p. 236.

primitive men," as a German critic, Richard Moritz Meyer,[1] puts it, "the poet is merely one of many whom a group experience has wrought up emotionally to such a pitch that a liberation from excitement is as strongly desired as the satisfaction of a physical need. From the group of mourners, the rejoicing, the enraged, the terrorstricken, there leaps forth one in whom the passion common to all has crystallized into intelligible speech; another leaps forth, perhaps a third. And each time the group of bystanders expresses its assent and inner liberation by cries and ululations. Here we observe that the poet has no existence separate from the tribe. The excitement once past, he is merely a tribal unit like any other."

Some such primitive, or, at least, highly naïve and homogeneous, social condition as this is to be assumed before communal composition is possible even in theory. How it might actually have operated in fact has been explained by many investigators.[2] After stating that ballads are both popular and primitive, Andrew Lang says of them:[3] "They date from times, and are composed by peoples who find, in a natural improvisation, a natural utterance of modulated and rhythmic speech, the appropriate relief of their emotions, in moments of high-wrought feeling or on solemn occasions."

The explanation given by Professor W. A. Neilson is longer and is exceedingly well phrased.[4] "There exists the evidence of the widespread practice of accompanying communal activity — in labor, ceremonial, or festal dance — with rhythmic utterances; the gradual growth of these utterances in definiteness of form; the practice of making them the medium of narrating some episode known to all, — for example, the story of some great deed accomplished by the hero whose death is being lamented, or the manner of the victory which is being celebrated, or some

---

[1] *Die Weltliteratur im zwanzigsten Jahrhundert,* transl. in L. Lewisohn, *A Modern Book of Criticism,* Boni and Liveright, 1919, p. 61.

[2] For example, G. L. Kittredge, F. B. Gummere, Andrew Lang, W. A. Neilson, W. M. Hart, L. McWatt, and others.

[3] "Ballads," *Encyclopaedia Britannica,* ninth ed.

[4] "Ballads," *Encyclopedia Americana,* 1918.

ludicrous incident in the season's labor happily finished, — the contribution of a new line or stanza now by this, now by that member of the dancing throng; the recurrent refrain sung by all; the final creation of a narrative song for which no one individual is responsible, but which is the expression of the thought and feeling of all.''

A Scottish writer thus describes the circumstances favorable to folk-song: [1] "Given, therefore, the provocative incident, add the beat of a drum, the throb of a string, the note of a pipe, the cry of the human voice, the slap of a hand or the tramp of the feet of the singers, and you find a great deal of the natural elements which make for the song of a people.''

Professor Kittredge, the leader among ballad authorities, interprets as follows the position of Professor Gummere, who was one of the staunchest and most influential advocates of the communal theory: [2] "'Folk' is a large word. It suggests a whole nation, or at all events a huge concourse of people. Let us abandon it, then, for the moment, and think rather of a small tribal gathering, assembled in very early times, or — what for the anthropologist amounts to the same thing — under very simple conditions of life, for the purpose of celebrating some occasion of common interest, — a successful hunt, or the return from a prosperous foray, or the repulse of a band of marauding strangers. The object of the meeting is known to all; the deeds which are to be sung, the dance which is to accompany and illustrate the singing, are likewise familiar to every one. There is no such diversity of intellectual interest as characterizes even the smallest company of civilized men. There is unity of feeling and a common stock, however slender, of ideas and traditions. The dancing and singing, in which all share, are so closely related as to be practically complementary parts of a single festal act. Here, now, we have the 'folk' of our discussion, reduced, as it were, to its lowest terms, a singing, dancing

---

[1] L. McWatt, *The Scottish Ballads and Ballad Writing*, Paisley, Alexander Gardner, Ltd., 1923.

[2] Kittredge, p. xix. See also his well-known reconstruction of "The Hangman's Tree," p. xxv.

throng subjected as a unit to a mental and emotional stimulus which is not only favorable to the production of poetry, but is almost certain to result in such production. And this is no fancy picture. It is the soberest kind of science, — a mere brief chapter of descriptive anthropology, for which authorities might be cited without number.

"Let us next consider the manner in which poetry (the word is of course used under pardon) is produced in such an assembly. Here again we can proceed upon just grounds of anthropological evidence. Different members of the throng, one after another, may chant each his verse, composed on the spur of the moment, and the sum of these various contributions makes a song. This is communal composition, though each verse, taken by itself, is the work of an individual. A song made in this way is no man's property and has no individual author. The 'folk' is its author."

## II. Contemporary American Instances

As described in these quoted passages, communal composition seems not only possible but plausible. In fact, something very much like it can be observed in contemporary American life. Naturally such instances are rare, and occur only under highly specialized social conditions. But they do occur. Life in the big lumber camps and on the cattle ranches, the religious fervor of Negro camp-meetings when "seeking" takes place, when testimony is given, and spirituals are sung, labor-gangs working at concerted tasks like digging or hauling or lifting — such are the conditions under which communal improvisation and group authorship take place. Humble examples these, but nevertheless interesting and significant.

For such light as they may serve to throw on a mooted process, and by way of illustration rather than argument, the following examples are offered for what they are worth. They vary greatly — in underlying conditions, method of production, and kind of product. Each, however, in its kind, seems to be an authentic instance of group authorship or improvisation by a throng.

*Among the Negroes*

It is probable that the way in which song is still improvised under certain conditions by certain classes of American Negroes resembles the theoretical process of communal authorship more closely than does any other contemporary American situation.[1]

It is a familiar sight in the South, for example, to see a gang of Negroes digging with pick-axes to the rhythm of a song, the workers all bringing their pick-axes down and grunting in unison at the end of every line or every other line. A favorite song for this purpose is the familiar "Lulu."

LULU

Lu - lu, my darl - in', Lu - lu, my dear,
That I don't love you Is a fool-ish i - dea.

> Lulu, my darlin',
> Lulu, my dear,
> That I don't love you
> Is a foolish idea.
>
> Six months in prison,
> Six months in jail;
> Send for my Lulu
> To go my bail.
>
> Build me a house
> On the mountain high;
> See my Lulu,
> As she passes by.

Sung to its simple tune with wailing rhythm, this song with its interminable array of stanzas will serve to dig by for hours. Now one, now another laborer sings a stanza, the other Negroes

[1] See on this point Joseph Hutchinson Smith, "Folk-Songs of the American Negro," *Sewanee Review*, April, 1924; and Newman I. White, *American Negro Folk-Songs*, Harvard University Press, 1928.

joining in if the words are familiar. After listening for some time to this song, during an interval of rest while the water-boy was circulating, a bystander asked the laborers how they remembered such a long song. They all nodded assent as one of them replied, "Don't remembuh it. We makes it up as we goes along."

The instant flexibility of such work-songs is surprising. A university dean was once listening to the improvisation of the song leader of a Negro road gang who were singing as they worked in front of his house. Wishing to hear the words more clearly, and possibly to take them down, the dean casually strolled out and took his seat on the rock wall bordering the road. He was thinking how intent upon their work the Negroes were, and how oblivious of his presence, when, without the slightest change of expression on their part or the loss of a beat of the rhythm, these words came floating to his ears:

> White man settin' on wall,
> White man settin' on wall,
> White man settin' on wall all day long,
> Wastin' his time, wastin' his time.[1]

Dr. E. C. L. Adams of South Carolina, who has made a close study of the Negro, has given the writer verbatim accounts of four Negro religious meetings [2] held in a small church in the country, each of which reveals group composition in a nascent stage, stopping just short of completion and permanence. The experience meeting and one of the Negro funeral sermons are here described in full.

## "The Wild Goose Nest"

[An experience meeting had been going on for some time, and both leader and congregation were at a high pitch of excitement. The leader, Brother Hickman, began calling for individual experiences and repentance.]

[1] Incident related in Howard W. Odum and Guy B. Johnson, *The Negro and his Songs*, University of North Carolina Press, 1925, pp. 2, 3.

[2] See E. C. L. Adams, *Congaree Sketches*, University of North Carolina Press, 1927: "Fragment of a Negro Sermon," "His Day is Done," "Wild Goose Nest," and "Jumping-Gut."

LEADER: Sister Peggy, what is your experience? Has you reach a determination in your travels?

SISTER PEGGY: Brother, I is. I travel a long distance and de road been rough and mighty dark, and nigh de end of de road I find a wild goose nest; and all de eggs but one is white, and it were black.

[*Congregation, chanting in unison*]:

> Wild goose nest,
> Wild goose nest,
> Wild goose nest.

LEADER: Sister, go back in de wilderness and pray some more. Go seek again till all de eggs in de wild goose nest is white.

[*Voices of sisters from different parts of the congregation*]:

> Wild goose nest,
> Wild goose nest,
> Wild goose nest.

[*Sister Peggy goes and returns.*]

SISTER PEGGY: Brother Hickman, I traveled to de wild goose nest, and de road been long and de road been rough, and I come to de wild goose nest.

[*Voices from the congregation*]: Tell us, sister!
[*All chanting*]:

> Wild goose nest,
> Wild goose nest,
> Wild goose nest,

> And de nest been soft with feathers
> From de wild goose breast,

> Wild goose breast,
> Wild goose breast,
> Wild goose breast,

> And all de eggs been white but one,
> And it still were black.

LEADER: Go back, Sister Peggy, go back in de wilderness and seek again for a determination. There is still work to be done. Go and pray and seek, sister, till all de eggs in de wild goose nest is white.

[*Congregation, in unison*]:

> Wild goose nest,
> Wild goose nest,
> Wild goose nest.

[*Sister Peggy goes and returns for the third time.*]

LEADER: What you find, Sister Peggy?

SISTER PEGGY: Brother, I have been to de wild goose nest, and all de eggs is white! All de eggs is white!

LEADER: My sister, you has reach a determination in your long travel and your labors is done. Rise, sister, your journey is done.

[*Congregation, in unison*]:

> Wild goose nest,
> Wild goose nest,
> Wild goose nest.

Even more striking is the reaction of the audience in the following account of a Negro funeral sermon, with its burden of rhythmic responses and choral repetitions. Another step in the same direction, and a new spiritual would have been perfected, "Oh, He Sleeps on the Bank of the River."

> Our Brother is dead,
> He rests from he labor
> An' he sleeps, —
>
> > [*Shrill voice of Sister*]: He sleeps,
> > Oh, he sleeps!
>
> Wey de tall pines grow,
>
> > [*Another voice*]: On the banks of a river.
>
> On the banks of a river.
>
> > [*Several voices*]: On the banks of a river.
>
> He trouble is done,
> He's left dis world
> On the wings of glory.
>
> > [*Voice*]: On the wings of glory!
>
> Out of life's storm,
>
> > [*Another voice*]: On the wings of glory!
>
> Out of life's darkness,
>
> > [*Several voices*]: On the wings of glory!

He sails in the light,
Of the Lamb.
Away from his troubles,
Away from the night.

> [*Congregation*]:    In the light!
> In the light!
> Of the Lamb.

He's gone to the kingdom above,
In the raiment of angels,

> [*Voice of Sister*]:    In the raiment!
> In the raiment of angels!

To the region above,
An' he sleeps, —

> [*Voices chanting throughout congregation*]:    Oh, he sleeps, —
> Oh, he sleeps!
> On the banks of a river.

Wey de tall pines grow,
On the banks of a river.

> [*Congregation*]:   With the starry crowned angels,
> On the banks of a river.

An' the flowers is bloomin'
In the blood of the Lamb.

> [*Shrill voice of Sister is taken up by
> congregation chanting and swaying*]:    The blood of the Lamb!
> In the blood of the Lamb!

An' the birds is singin'
Wey de wind blows soft,
As the breath of an angel,
An' he sleeps!
Wey de tall pines grow,
On the banks of a river.

> [*Voice*]:   An' he sleeps!
> [*Another voice*]:   Wey de tall pines grow.

An' his sperrit is guarded,

> [*Several voices*]:   On the banks of a river.

By a flaming-faced angel.

> [*Sister*]:   Yes, Jesus, of a flaming-faced angel
> On the banks of a river.

Standing on mountains of rest.
An' he sleeps wey de tall pines grow,
On the banks of a river.

> [*Congregation*]:   Oh, he sleeps!
> He sleeps!

The united emotional adaptability and instant rhythmic responsiveness displayed by a Negro audience on such occasions as this seem at first to be beyond the bounds of possibility. Entirely natural was the surprised comment of an observer who for the first time had been present at a Negro funeral: "Why, it sounded exactly like they had practised it all up beforehand!"

Many similar illustrations could be given from the making and singing of Negro spirituals.[1] The spiritual is properly not static or final, but dynamic and growing, for it is the creature of oral tradition and fully exemplifies every possibility of variation associated with oral tradition and communal transmission.

New spirituals are constantly being made, either by individuals, or by groups, spontaneously. Individual authorship has been thus described by two leading Southern authorities.[2]

"Among the lowly Negro folk of the South, the making of spirituals is still a reality. Every community has its 'composers.' Often they are supposed to possess some special gift of the 'spirit.' From sermon, prayer, and crude folk wisdom they draw ideas and inspiration for their compositions. Sometimes the results are pathetic, but not infrequently there springs up a song which would compare favorably with the old spirituals."

It is the group authorship of spirituals, however, that we are concerned with here. There are many instances of group authorship on record, and it can still be observed under favorable circumstances.

An emotionally charged atmosphere (as religious worship regularly charges it among all but the most sophisticated Negroes), a striking, rhythmic phrase from preacher, leader, or worshipper, and the thing is done. One of the most beautiful of recent spirituals was a spontaneous outburst of petition to the great "Maussa" after the terrific cyclone of 1911 in South Carolina, built around the refrain appeal, "Lord, don' let de win' blow here no mo'." [3] And during the World War a similarly tense

[1] See also J. W. Johnson, *The Book of American Negro Spirituals*, preface, p. 21.

[2] Howard W. Odum and Guy B. Johnson, *Negro Workaday Songs*, University of North Carolina Press, 1926, p. 189.

[3] Printed in N. G. J. Ballanta, *Saint Helena Island Spirituals*, No. 39.

situation produced a like result. As described by a Negro worshipper on that occasion: "Somebody shout out, 'O Lord, we gwine t'row dat Kizer down,' an' den somebody else catch 'em an' t'row 'em back, an' befo' you know it de whole chu'ch was a-rockin' an' a-prayin'. It was a gran' hymn."

Two similar instances are described by Professors Odum and Johnson:[1] "A Negro preacher recently reached a climax in his discourse in the phrase, 'Oh, with the wings of the morning, I'd fly to that heavenly land.' He repeated this a number of times and made gestures with his arms suggestive of flying. His black robe added to the forcefulness of the suggestion and the impression became a part of the song of that church. . . . If a single personality dominates the whole in an expression that appeals to the present sense of fitness, he is the author of a new song. For example, a visiting minister once shouted out during such a scene: 'Oh, the hearse-wheel a-rollin' an' the graveyard opening — ha, ha,' but got no further; for his refrain was taken up by the chorus, and the next day saw a new version of the well-known song."

Group origin is also suggested by Thomas Wentworth Higginson for the song, "O, de Ole Nigger-Driver!" which he reproduces in his pioneer article on "Negro Spirituals" in *The Atlantic Monthly*, June, 1867.

### An Indian Instance

The best instance of communal composition among the Indians seems to be the one that Miss Louise Pound cites in a recent attack on the communal theory.[2] "*Composition of Songs.* It was said by several singers that they 'heard a song in their sleep,' sang it, and either awoke to find themselves singing it aloud, or remembered it and were able to sing it. No information

---

[1] *The Negro and his Songs*, p. 32.
[2] "The Term: 'Communal,'" *Publications Modern Language Association*, vol. xxxix (1924), pp. 440–454. Her citation is from Frances Densmore's *Northern Ute Music*, 1922, p. 26, a volume issued as Bulletin 76 of the Publications of the American Bureau of Ethnology.

was attained on any other method of producing songs. In this connection the writer [Miss Densmore] desires to record an observation on musical composition among the Sioux. A song was sung at a gathering and she remarked: 'That is different from any Sioux song I have ever heard, it has so many peculiarities.' The interpreter replied, 'That song was composed recently by several men working together. Each man suggested something and they put it all together in the song.' This is the only instance of coöperation in the composition of an Indian song that has been observed, adds Miss Densmore."

### Among North Carolina Mountaineers

Two examples of group composition of a song in mountain communities of North Carolina were recently described to the writer by Miss Tressie Pierce of Columbia, S. C. In the first case, a young mountain girl some years ago was accidentally burned to death by the explosion of a lamp. In the house where the body was lying the night before the funeral, a group of her friends gathered in a room and together composed the following song, and sang it the next day at the grave. The community, which is near Taylorsville, N. C., is one where fondness for and skill in folk-song still linger to an unusual extent.

1. Gentle zephyrs, blow ye lightly,
   O'er the place, where sleeps the dead;
   Where the moon-beams sparkle brightly,
   Hovering around that narrow bed.

#### Refrain

Far where yonders Ivy creep,
   Is the place sweet Ella sleeps;
Far where yonders Ivy creep,
   Is the place sweet Ella sleeps.

2. When the night of death came o'er her,
   And her eyes began to close,
   Happy dreams went on before her,
   Calling her to sweet repose.

3. Then she fell in slumber deep,
    Leaving us below to weep;
  Then she fell in slumber deep,
    Leaving us below to weep.

4. Gentle zephyrs, whisper lightly,
    O'er that sacred, hallowed spot,
  Where the moon-beams sparkle brightly,
    Ah, it cannot be forgot.

The second instance is much like the first, both in origin and in result. A bride of two months was murdered near Stony-point, N. C. Intense local excitement was aroused by the event. When it was discovered that the murderer was the husband, a group of the young friends and schoolmates of the young couple gathered, and together composed a song of lament containing ten stanzas. The first stanza and the chorus will suffice to give its general character, which, as might be expected, is prevailingly sentimental and resembles closely the tone of the preceding song.

### BESSIE COMBS

It was one beautiful night in May,
  Sweet Bessie was singing in glee.
She did not know it was in Reuben's heart
  To take her sweet life away.

#### Chorus

O Bessie, my darling, come home;
  Bid Reuben alone adieu.
His hands are stained with your own blood;
  He can never come up to you.

### Among Texas Cowboys

Mr. John A. Lomax of Texas, the chief collector of South-western folk-songs and cowboy ballads, speaks of group composition among the cowboys as an established fact.[1] "There has sprung up in America," he says, "a considerable body of folk-song called by courtesy 'ballads,' which in their authorship, in the social conditions under which they were produced, in the

[1] Pound, pp. 214, 215.

spirit which gives them life, resemble the genuine ballads sung
by our English and Scottish ancestors long before there was an
American people. 'The Ballad of the Boll Weevil' and 'The
Ballad of the Old Chisholm Trail,' and other songs in my collection similar to these, are absolutely known to have been composed by groups of people whose community life made their
thinking similar, and present valuable corroborative evidence
of the theory advanced by Professor Gummere and Professor
Kittredge concerning the origin of the ballads from which come
those now contained in the great Child collection."

Ex-President Roosevelt was much interested in Mr. Lomax's
work and wrote, in a personal letter to him in 1910, that [1] "there
is something very curious in the reproduction here on this new
continent of essentially the conditions of ballad-growth which
obtained in mediaeval England."

### In the American Expeditionary Force

Under the title "Communal Composition of Ballads in the
A. E. F.," a returned soldier describes an evening of group-song
production to the ubiquitous tune of "Hinkie Dinkie, Parlez
vous." [2]

"The day came for our unit to come homeward. During the
three weeks of waiting at St. Nazaire, most of us did little but
sit and talk. One rainy evening, when the lights were so weak
that no one could read, a group of about eight men gathered at
one end of the barracks, and spent their time in singing. After
the usual round of old favorites, they commenced vying with
one another in composing words to 'Hinkie Dinkie,' with slurs
at less popular members of the organization. Not more than
three or four verses had been composed, before men outside of
the group began to collect around and to suggest further names
to be used. Instantly some one of the original eight produced a
rhyme. I was surprised often at the accuracy with which in two
lines the eccentricity of a character was hit off. Laughter and

---

[1] See facsimile frontispiece, John A. Lomax, *Cowboy Songs*, Macmillan Co., 1919.
[2] Atcheson L. Hench, *J. A. F. L.*, xxxiv, 386–389.

applause spurred the brighter ones to harder thinking, so that
in the process of an hour some twelve or fifteen men had been
noted and characterized. It was natural, too, that one man
should show himself quicker at rhymes than another. Before
seven or eight stanzas had been composed, one young boy
stepped far ahead of the rest in his productions; but his ability
showed itself only because he had several men pursuing him for
the honors.

"Had I been quick enough to realize the significance of the
performance, I should have snatched paper and copied down the
verses, but not till the next day did the thought occur to me
that I had witnessed communal composition."

### A "Tall Tale" from Missouri

A case of the group-versifying of an amusing "tall tale" recently came to the notice of Professor Albert H. Tolman of the
University of Chicago.[1] The starting-point was the fairly well-
known extravaganza on the size and fierceness of mosquitoes
(this time in Missouri). Professor Tolman's informant gave the
following account of the composition of the song: "This tale
amused the men so much that one night one of the men sang a
version of the song I sent you. My father said it took well, and,
joking and laughing, the men added some and revised some. He
was sitting in the room reading, and jotted the song down in the
final form agreed upon by the men. He does n't know whether
the first man had written the first version down or not, but the
others just improvised words to fit the first one's tune. One
man . . . contributed [who] could neither read nor write.
About three men did most of the work, although there were
several more there."

The words of the song run thus:

> We was loggin' in Kentucky
>    With Jerry and Joe,
> Draggin' up the timber
>    An' makin' things go.

---

[1] Albert H. Tolman, "The Group-Authorship of Ballads," *P. M. L. A.*, xlii, 428–
432.

Jerry and Joe
  Was oxen white,
Pastured in a gulch
  Every summer night.

One mornin' early
  Bob went to get the yoke,
But he could n't find 'em,
  No matter where he'd look.

He called out the loggers,
  Off-bear and sawyer, too,
For, without the oxen
  He did n't know what to do.

But at last they heard a bell
  Way up in a tree,
An' there they saw a skeeter
  As big as could be.

They saw he'd eaten Jerry
  Early that morn;
He was pickin' his teeth
  With Jerry's horn.

But still he was hungry;
  The boys say so;
He was ringin' Jerry's bell
  To call up Joe.

They hunted and they hunted;
  They looked high and low;
But all they could find
  Was the ox named Joe.

### In a South Carolina High School

One of the slower English sections of the first year of a city high school was studying ballads, and one day the teacher proposed to the class the device of writing a ballad together. The class assented enthusiastically. The teacher left everything to them — choice of subject, length, metre, method of treatment, refrain, and so forth. The pupils entered wholeheartedly into the project. For the subject they chose the story of "Little Red Riding Hood," and, for the refrain, settled on "Don't stop in the woods to play!" Suggestions for words, phrases, and lines came rapidly from all parts of the room, and, with the teacher acting mainly as recording secretary, a ballad of nine stanzas was composed in less than an hour.[1]   The first two stanzas run:

> Red Riding Hood to her grandmother's went
>     Upon a bright spring day.
> Her mother dressed her and said to her,
>     "Don't stop in the woods to play!
> If you talk to strangers that you meet
>     Upon this bright spring day,
> I may never be able to dress you again,
>     So don't stop in the woods to play."
>
> She had not gone one mile but twa
>     When she stopped in the woods to play —
> And up there came a big gray wolf,
>     Who would show her a shorter way —
> As she looked at the wolf with his big old mouth,
>     She heard her mother say,
> "Never talk to strangers in the woods —
>     Don't stop in the woods to play!"

Interesting features of this composition are, first, that this group of pupils was below medium grade in ability-performance; and, second, that the putting together of the lines was done spontaneously and widely from all parts of the room.

### III.  The Other Side

To take a brief glance at the other side of the argument, those who oppose the communal theory hold that the chief objection to it is this: while communal composition not only is possible in theory, but is actually being carried on in sporadic fashion today, its products are often fragmentary and always crude.  From the shreds and patches actually produced in authentic instances of communal improvisation, it is a far cry to the consecutiveness and climactic unity of "Sir Patrick Spens" and "Bonny James Campbell," or even to ballads like "The Hangman's Tree," or "Barbara Allen."  The mill of the people still grinds and it grinds exceeding small, but it grinds chaff and not wheat.

---

    Information furnished by Miss Frances W. Sylvan of the Columbia (S. C.) High School.

One of the most uncompromising opponents of the communal theory in Great Britain is the Scottish scholar, T. F. Henderson. With considerable vigor and not a little sarcasm, on the one hand he rejects communal authorship, and on the other insists that oral transmission always results in ballad degeneration and debasement. Typical of his attitude is the following comment on one of the older ballads, "Robyn and Gandeleyn":[1] "Any one who chooses to believe that the genius of the improvising throng and the chance of blind tradition are, together, sufficient to account for the production of this fine ballad, may be left in the possession of his conviction; my own mental faculties will not permit me to conceive its possibility."

The leading American anti-communalist is Miss Louise Pound of Nebraska University. She sums up the case for the opposition in this fashion:[2] "But who has certainly, not conjecturally, pointed out for America a good ballad, that is, verse-story, which did originate communally and has also obtained widespread diffusion?

"The English and Scottish ballads should no longer be inevitably related to primitive singing and dancing throngs, improvising and collaborating. We cannot look upon creations of such length, structure, coherence, finish, artistic value, adequacy of expression, as emerging from the communal improvisation of simple, uneducated folk throngs. This view might serve so long as we had not clear evidence before us as to the kind of thing that the improvising folk-muse is able to create. When we see what is the best the latter can do, under no less favorable conditions, at the present time, we remain skeptical as to the power of the mediaeval rustics and villagers. The mere fact that the mediaeval throngs are supposed by many scholars to have danced while they sung, whereas modern cowboys, lumbermen, ranchmen, or Negroes do not, should not have endowed the mediaeval muse with such striking superiority of product."

[1] For a full statement of his views, see Henderson, chap. 3, "The Origin and Authorship of Ballads."

[2] Pound, p. 161.

"It has often been pointed out that in the Southern Appalachians exist isolated communities, unlettered and cut off for a hundred years from traffic with the rest of the world; and these communities still entertain themselves with traditional song. Conditions are ideal for the creation of communal ballads, according to the orthodox theory. Yet their investigators have not found that they have any body of song of their own creation, whether pure lyrics or ballads. They still sing the English and Scottish ballads brought over by their ancestors. Self-created songs about their own life are conspicuously wanting. The Southwestern cowboys perhaps live as communal a life as any in our period, possibly they are more literate than the mountaineers, but they are little more creative. The bulk of their song entered their circles from the outside world. Where they have songs concerning themselves, they are fitted to familiar melodies, and (at least the songs which have value or memorableness) are adaptations of already existent material. The best cowboy songs having claim to originality may be traced to minor poets. The cowboy songs which are nearest to genuine communal creations are those of weakest quality, are not narrative, and are in character most ephemeral." [1]

"As a critical hypothesis the whole communal prepossession has led mainly into misconception and misvaluation; its service (for service of a sort it is) has been to rouse an interest and an industry in its support which have only succeeded in demonstrating its futility. In other words, it is honorably shelved by its own inability to stand the test of substantial evidence." [2]

The general purpose of the foregoing treatment of communal composition is explanatory rather than argumentative. Miss Pound has been quoted because she is such a consistent and formidable opponent of the communal theory. The communalists of course do not agree with her that the theory "is honorably shelved by its own inability to stand the test of substantial

[1] Louise Pound, "The Term: 'Communal,'" *P. M. L. A.*, xxxix (June, 1924), 449.
[2] *Ibid.*, p. 444.

evidence." Rather do they conceive it as exclaiming with Johnnie Armstrong:

> Saying, "Fight on, my merry men all,
>     I am a little hurt but I am not slain;
> I will lay me down for to bleed a while,
>     Then I'll rise and fight with you again."

The weakness of the anti-communalists' attack lies in the facts that it is negative in character and that it rests upon analogy. First, as to its negative quality: the attackers point out that there has not been brought to light a single modern ballad resembling the Child or Grundtvig ballads which is clearly the result of communal authorship or group improvisation. The communalists grant this, but reply that neither have the anti-communalists brought to light a modern ballad resembling the traditional ballads which is the result of individual authorship or of any other kind of authorship. In other words, such ballads are not being produced any longer anywhere in the world. This fact, however, as an argument, could be used just as logically against individual authorship as against communal composition.

Second, as to analogy: the anti-communal argument, stripped to its essentials, is that no modern community, not even one of naïve, isolated, and homogeneous character, such as a mountain cove or a cattle-ranch, has produced communally a ballad resembling the Child ballads. Therefore, no community, anywhere or at any time, did so or could have done so.

This is stretching analogy to the breaking-point; and at best, analogy is stronger as illustration than as argument. Arguing by analogy usually consists in looking for resemblances and in ignoring differences; and in general the argument from analogy has little validity unless the resemblances between the familiar object and the unknown are shown to be due to the same cause. The differences between conditions surrounding peasant life in England and Scotland, say in 1350 or 1400, and those surrounding community life anywhere in America, say in 1850 or 1900, are so manifold and essential that significant comparison would seem almost out of the question.

The communal theory is only a theory, not a proved formula for ballad production. The communalists hold, however, that no equally satisfactory substitute has ever been found, with the implied invitation, "If you know of a better 'ole, go to it."

# IV

## COMMUNAL TRANSMISSION

### I. IN TRADITIONAL BALLADS

COMMUNAL composition "Das Volk dichtet" is the theory that most completely explains both the impersonality and the other characteristics of the ballad. But those who cannot credit this theory think that ballad characteristics are accounted for also by the fact that ballads were circulated and preserved by oral tradition. This means that ballads lived by passing from mouth to ear, from singer to listener, from being heard to being remembered, spreading from community to community, from section to section, from father to son, from mother to daughter, in an ever-widening circle of space and time, and all without the scratch of a pen or a line of type.

This process may fairly be called communal transmission. It naturally resulted in the filtering off or straining out of all traces of personal authorship and touches of individuality. Only impersonality and lack of self-consciousness remained. For, passing as it were through successive time-layers and space-layers of folk-consciousness, ballads have come out recolored and re-created after the likeness of the people, with no personal image or superscription remaining.

Oral transmission accounts, too, not only for the constant fluctuations both in ballad texts and in ballad melodies, but also for the large number of versions and variants, and for the presence of many local improvisations and additions.

The transformation wrought by oral tradition in a ballad, from the time it is composed until it is recorded in writing, has been thus outlined by Professor Kittredge: [1]

[1] Kittredge, p. xvii.

As it passes from singer to singer it is changing unceasingly.  Old stanzas are dropped and new ones are added;  rhymes are altered;  the names of the characters are varied;  portions of other ballads work their way in;  the catastrophe may be transformed completely. Finally, if the tradition continues for two or three centuries, as it frequently does continue, the whole linguistic complexion of the piece may be so modified with the development of the language in which it is composed that the original author would not recognize his work if he heard it recited.  Taken collectively, these processes of oral tradition amount to a second act of composition, of an inextricably complicated character, in which many persons share (some consciously, others without knowing it), which extends over many generations and much geographical space, and which may be as efficient a cause of the ballad in question as the original creative act of the individual author.  It would be a great mistake to regard the results of what we may call, for want of a better term, collective composition, as identical with the corruptions of scribes and editors in the case of a classical text.  Individually they are sometimes indistinguishable from such corruptions, but in the aggregate they amount to a distinct kind of authorship which every student of popular literature is obliged to recognize, not only as actually operative in the production of ballads, but as legitimate.  They may even result in the production of new ballads to which no individual author can lay claim, so completely is the initial act of creative authorship overshadowed by the secondary act of collective composition.

Or, as Neilson concisely remarks,[1]

The life of a modern poem begins when it is committed to paper; a ballad then begins to die.  It lives only while it is still being transmitted orally from generation to generation, receiving from each its stamp.

With these expressions may be compared the opinion of the English authority on folk-song, Cecil J. Sharp:[2]

Suffice it to say that the writer is a stout upholder of the communal theory of origin;  that he believes that the nature of the folksong and its history can be satisfactorily explained only on that hypothesis; that the most typical qualities of the folksong have been laboriously acquired during its journey down the ages, in the course of which its individual angles and irregularities have been rubbed and smoothed

[1] "Ballads," *Encyclopedia Americana*, 1918.
[2] *One Hundred English Folksongs*, Oliver Ditson Co., 1916.  Introd., p. xiv.  It is clear from other passages in his Introduction that, when Mr. Sharp speaks of the communal theory of origins, he is referring to transmission, not to composition.

away, just as the pebble on the seashore has been rounded by the action of the waves; that the suggestions, unconsciously made by individual singers, have at every stage of the evolution of the folk-song been weighed and tested by the community, and accepted or rejected by their verdict; and that the life history of the folksong has been one of continuous growth and development, always tending to approximate to a form which should be at once congenial to the taste of the community and expressive of its feelings, aspirations, and ideals.

In a recent article on ballads [1] Professor G. H. Gerould of Princeton calls attention to the significant fact that, of the 305 ballads in Child's collection, no fewer than 65 are represented by different versions of distinguished merit and high poetic charm, not one of which could be well spared. In other words, what we have termed communal transmission has produced, not one excellent version, but several excellent versions, with marked individual differences, but all of unusual poetic value.

It would be interesting [as Professor Kittredge points out [2]], if we could have every one of Mr. Child's three hundred and five ballads exactly as it came from the lips or hands of its first composer; but such versions, if we could arrive at them, would not cancel the variants that have come down to us. Oral transmission and its concomitants are not the accidents of the ballad, they are essential to it; they are constituent elements of its very nature. Without them the ballad would not be the ballad.

To the same effect Dr. C. Alphonso Smith remarked, apropos of an unusually complete Virginia variant of "Barbara Allen": [3]

It is possible, of course, that this better-constructed version may be as old as any version known to us. All that we know of any printed and dated British version is that at that particular time the ballad was intercepted by an interested collector. It may have been a hundred or two hundred years old before it got itself printed, it may have already crossed over to America, and it may have existed all this time in a score of variants or versions. The collector halts only one of them, and that only long enough to get a copy. The other versions and the version from which the copy has been made pursue their way from lip to lip and from century to century, though the printed version has now an advantage. When it comes into con-

---

[1] Gerould, pp. 15–28.   [2] Kittredge, p. xviii.   [3] Smith, pp. 120, 122.

tact with what may really be an older oral version or with a later
oral version or with the now changed oral version that was once its
own unembodied self, it is apt to put on airs, merely because, having
ink in its veins, it has been associating with books and bookish folk.
But the chances are that it is merely a case of arrested development.
It is only a pailful of stagnant water once dipped from a running
stream.

The first version, if we could catch it hot from the lips of the composing throng, would not, through mere priority, be one whit more
authentic or authoritative than the latest version, provided the
latest version was also the product of the people.  Let us think of a
ballad as a thought or deed or situation or incident or motif adventur-
ing forth to get itself artistically expressed.  The standard version,
if one insists on the word, is merely the most adequate incarnation
that the wandering concept is fortunate enough to assume: it is the
best version, whether made in Great Britain or America, whether the
child of the fifteenth or the twentieth century.

A striking example of this is to be found in the two versions
of "The Queen of Elfan's Nourice" quoted and compared by
Professor W. M. Hart.[1]  The first version is that printed by
Child from the *Ballad Book* of C. K. Sharpe, who collected his
ballads early in the last century from the mouths of nurses,
dairymaids, and tenants' daughters.  Sharpe's version is obvi-
ously fragmentary; lines and stanzas are missing, and, at the
close, three stanzas from another ballad, "Thomas Rymer," are
appended.

The second version [as Professor Hart explains] was taken down
in 1906 from the recitation of Mrs. McLeod of Dumfries, Scotland,
who was then visiting relatives at Lake Mills, Wisconsin.  It is undoubtedly traditional, as the reciter could not read or write, nor could
her parents before her.  Her version is superior to the other. . . .
So far as it goes, it is complete; it makes the situation thoroughly
intelligible; it shows that the lowing of the cow is really an elf-call;
and it does not include the stanzas from "Thomas Rymer."  Thus,
though taken down perhaps a hundred years after the first version,
the second version is clearly the older, for it is nearer the original
form.

[1] Hart, Introd., pp. 46, 47.

## II. In Contemporary Songs

The effects of communal transmission,[1] as outlined thus far, seem to most ballad students to account satisfactorily for the ballads as we have them.   The communal extremists, however, still insist on communal composition as well as on communal transmission.   That is, as they see them, ballads are not merely popular by destination but also popular by origins.   The crux of the situation has been clearly stated by Professor Gummere in these words:[2]

If, however, one simply defines the popular ballad as a narrative lyric which in course of oral tradition has come into favor with the people, then there is nothing but the law of copyright and the personal fame of Mr. Kipling which could serve at some future day to exclude his "Danny Deever" from a collection of English popular ballads or to differentiate it from "Hobie Noble" and "Jock o' the Side."

To this most communalists would answer: set "Danny Deever" to a really catchy tune, give it a couple of decades' start in oral tradition, and it would feel perfectly at home in the best traditional company.

Nor is such an answer theoretical.   Instances of exactly that kind of thing are repeatedly happening in oral tradition.   Three in particular seem especially significant, — "The Ballad of the Oysterman," "De Fust Banjo," and "The Good Old Rebel," — and will be described in detail.

"The Ballad of the Oysterman" was written in 1830 by Oliver Wendell Holmes.   As explained by the editors of a recent book of Maine folk-songs,[3] however, it did not long remain Dr. Holmes's own production.

The ballad-sheet printer and the cheap songbook-maker promptly pirated it and bore it off, without bow to copyright or acknowledgment of any sort; it became anonymous immediately and the Folk

---

[1] For a thoughtful analysis of these effects, see John Robert Moore's article, "The Influence of Transmission on the English Ballads," *Modern Language Review*, vol. xi, no. 4 (October, 1916), pp. 385–408.

[2] Gummere, p. 14.

[3] Fannie H. Eckstorm and May W. Smyth, *Minstrelsy of Maine*, Houghton Mifflin Co., 1927, pp. 266, 267.

adopted it joyously, and still are singing it occasionally.  We have
picked up one copy of it fitted out with a comic ending and a "tol-de-
rol-de-riddle-de-ride-o" refrain which would have grieved the fastidi-
ous soul of Dr. Holmes. . . .  Hardly more than six years after he
had written "The Ballad of the Oysterman" it was well on its way to
alteration.  In the John Hay Library of Brown University we have
found a local broadside with the imprint of "42 North Main Street,
Providence," which by its black latticed border shows that it must
have been printed about 1836.  It has eight stanzas, one having been
added to meet the popular taste, and in various ways it has been
revised.  Evidently the word "metamorphosed" proved difficult, for
it is changed into "metamphrosed" — which in later copies is dropped
out entirely, together with the classical reference to Leander and the
Hellespont.  Holmes's delicately diffusive opening, "It was a tall
young oysterman," becomes the direct, "There was a tall young
oysterman"; the young lady, instead of being "wide awake," declares
herself "up to snuff" and "chucks a brickbat," instead of "throws a
pebble," into the water; and the notable changes in the sixth stanza
of the original are begun — all this probably within six years of the
composition of the poem.

The question to debate is, Did the Folk, by their adoption of "The
Ballad of the Oysterman," make it anonymous — like the other old
ballads?

"De Fust Banjo" first appeared in print as lines 184–227 of
Irwin Russell's pioneer Negro dialect poem, "Christmas Night
in the Quarters," 1878.  This poem had, and still has, wide circulation and popularity.

In 1916, with the title "Old Noah," it was sent in as a folk-
song to Professor J. H. Cox, who was then making a collection of the folk-songs of West Virginia.  Its folk genealogy is
unimpeachable.  It is described as "contributed by Mr. Decker
Toney, Queen's Ridge, Wayne County; learned from his mother
who learned it from Sarah Vance, who learned it from her uncle,
Riley Vance."  In Professor Cox's collection [1] it is printed in
seventeen four-line stanzas.  For purposes of comparison, parallel passages from the beginning and end of both versions may
be quoted.

[1] Cox, No. 181.

### De Fust Banjo

by Irwin Russell

Go 'way, fiddle! folks is tired o' hearin' you a-squawkin',
Keep silence fur yo' betters! — don't you heah de banjo talkin'?
About de possum's tail she's gwine to lecter, ladies, listen! —
About de ha'r whut is n't dar, an' why de ha'r is missin'.

.    .    .    .    .    .    .    .    .

Now, Ham, de only nigger whut wuz runnin' on de packet,
Got lonesome in de barber-shop, an' c'u'd n't stan' de racket.

.    .    .    .    .    .    .    .    .

De 'possum had as fine a tail as dis dat I's a-singin';
De ha'r 's so long an' thick an' strong, — des fit fur banjo-stringin';
Dat nigger shaved 'em off as short as wash-day dinner graces;
An' sorted ob 'em by de size, f'om little E's to basses.

He strung her, tuned her, struck a jig, — 't wuz "Nebber min' de
    wedder," —
She soun' like forty-lebben bands a-playin' all togedder;
Some went to pattin'; some to dancin'; Noah called de figgers;
An' Ham he sot an' knocked de tune, de happiest ob niggers!

Now, sence dat time — it's mighty strange — dere's not de slightes'
    showin'
Ob any ha'r at all upon de possum's tail a-growin';
An' curi's, too, dat nigger's ways; his people neber los' 'em —
Fur whar you finds de nigger — dar's de banjo an' de 'possum!

### Old Noah

Cox's *Folk-Songs of the South*

Go way, old fiddle,
    People is tired of your squawking!
Come listen to your better;
    Don't you hear the banjo talking?

It's about the possum's tail,
    I'll let you ladies listen —
Whilst the hair it is not there,
    And why it is so missing.

.    .    .    .    .    .    .    .    .

Then Sam, our only nigger,
  Was sailing in the package,
Got lonesome in the barber shop
  And could n't stand the racket.

.    .    .    .    .    .    .    .

Of course the possum he is here,
  Just as fine as I am singing;
The hide on the possum's tail
  Will do for the banjo stringing.

He took the hide, he shaved it out
  From little east to graces;
He tuned her up, he strung her up,
  From little *e* to basses.

He tuned her up and struck a jig,
  Saying, "Never mind the weather!"
She sounded like eleven banjos,
  Playing all together.

Some got to patting, some got to dancing,
  Old Noah called the figure;
But the happiest man in our crowd
  Was Sam, our only nigger.

Almost exactly parallel is the case of "The Good Old Rebel." This pungent bit of war verse has been attributed to several sources, but it is reasonably certain that it was written just after the Civil War by Innes Randolph (1837–1887).[1] It has been published at least five times.[2]

Its pungency and quotability floated it off, likewise, on a separate career in oral tradition, where it still leads an ear-to-mouth existence, parallel to, but entirely apart from, its authorized life in print. Thus it has been taken down no fewer than three

[1] See *Poems by Innes Randolph, Compiled by his Son* [Harold Randolph] *from the Original Manuscript*, Baltimore, Williams and Wilkins Co., 1898.

In the preface, p. 5, Mr. Harold Randolph says: "The 'Good Old Rebel' was written shortly afterward [after active hostilities ceased], while reconstruction held sway in the South."

[2] Fagan, *Southern War Songs*, New York, 1890; *Poems of Innes Randolph*, Baltimore, 1898, edited by his son, Harold Randolph; Davidson, *Cullings from the Confederacy*, Washington, 1903; Ellinger, *The Southern War Poetry of the Civil War*, p. 134; Wallace and Frances Rice, *The Humbler Poets*, Chicago, 1911.

times as a folk-song: once in Texas, where it found a place in Lomax's *Cowboy Ballads;*[1] once in West Virginia, where it was included in Cox's *Folk-Songs of The South;*[2] and once in Mississippi.[3]

Both because the poem is worth quoting on its own account and in order that comparison may be made, the original Innes Randolph version as printed by his son is given alongside of the oral version recovered by Lomax.

### The Good Old Rebel

#### by Innes Randolph

Oh, I'm a good old Rebel,
   Now that's just what I am,
For this "fair Land of Freedom"
   I do not care a damn.
I'm glad I fit against it —
   I only wish we'd won,
And I don't want no pardon
   For anything I've done.

I hates the Constitution,
   This great Republic, too,
I hates the Freedmen's Buro,
   In uniforms of blue.
I hates the nasty eagle,
   With all his brag and fuss;
The lyin', thievin' Yankees
   I hates 'em wuss and wuss.

I hate the Yankee Nation
   And everything they do;
I hate the Declaration
   Of Independence, too.
I hates the glorious Union,
   'T is dripping with our blood;
I hates the striped banner —
   I fit it all I could.

[1] Page 94. For another current oral variant, see John A. Lomax, *J. A. F. L.,* xxviii, 11.

[2] Page 281.

[3] See Arthur Palmer Hudson, "Ballads and Songs from Mississippi," *J. A. F. L.,* xxxix, 172.

I followed old Mars' Robert
  For four years, near about,
Got wounded in three places,
  And starved at Point Lookout.
I cotch the roomatism
  A-campin' in the snow,
But I killed a chance of Yankees —
  I'd like to kill some mo'.

Three hundred thousand Yankees
  Is stiff in Southern dust;
We got three hundred thousand
  Before they conquered us.
They died of Southern fever
  And Southern steel and shot;
I wish it was three millions
  Instead of what we got.

I can't take up my musket
  And fight 'em now no more,
But I ain't a-goin' to love 'em,
  Now that is sartin sure.
And I don't want no pardon
  For what I was and am;
I won't be reconstructed,
  And I don't care a damn.

## For I'm a Good Old Rebel

Lomax's *Cowboy Songs*

Oh, I'm a good old rebel, that's what I am;
And for this land of freedom, I don't care a damn,
I'm glad I fought again her, I only wish we'd won,
And I don't axe any pardon for anything I've done.

I served with old Bob Lee, three years about,
Got wounded in four places and starved at Point Lookout;
I caught the rheumatism a-campin' in the snow,
But I killed a chance of Yankees and wish I'd killed some mo'.

    For I'm a good old rebel, *etc.*

I hate the constitooshin, this great republic too;
I hate the mouty eagle, an' the uniform so blue;
I hate their glorious banner, an' all their flags an' fuss,
Those lyin', thievin' Yankees, I hate 'em wuss an' wuss.

    For I'm a good old rebel, *etc.*

I won't be re-constructed! I'm better now than them;
And for a carpet-bagger, I don't give a damn;
So I'm off for the frontier, soon as I can go,
I'll prepare me a weapon and start for Mexico.

For I'm a good old rebel, *etc.*

What has happened to "The Ballad of the Oysterman," "De Fust Banjo," and "The Good Old Rebel" shows how easy it is for an individual-author version to float off into oral tradition and be taken over by the people.

The reverse process also occurs frequently, in which a genuine folk-song is taken over by an individual author, is touched up, and is claimed as his own. A song-hit of a former generation, "There is a tavern in our town," is an interesting case in point. Mr. S. Baring-Gould, the British folk-song authority, thus explains its genesis:[1]

"There is a tavern in our town" is an introduction from America, and has become popular. Now this happens to be one of our folk-songs. It begins:

"A brisk young miner [or sailor] courted me;
He stole away my liberty;
He stole my heart with my good will
For all his faults I love him still."

Then follows the verse, "There is an ale-house in our town," *etc.* Some Cornish miners sang this in the States, it was heard by a musician, who touched it up a little, added a chorus, cut out some verses not perhaps objectionable, but undesirable, and now it is hailed with a hearty greeting as an American ditty.

Contemporary oral transmission, however, offers instances not only of individual-author-to-folk and folk-to-individual-author influences, but also of how stanzas, situations, and incidents are borrowed back and forth in the different songs. Mr. R. W. Gordon, who has a wide acquaintance with the vicissitudes of current popular songs, comments as follows on this

[1] S. Baring-Gould and H. Fleetwood Sheppard, *A Garland of Country Song*, Methuen and Co., London, 1895, Introd., p. vi.

point in connection with a current variant of "The Game of Coon-Can":[1]

Here is the best of a number of different versions of "The Game of Coon-Can" that have come in to the department during the past two years. It comes from W. F. B., who picked it up "from a 'blowed-in-the-glass stiff' in the 'jungles' at Livingston, Montana."

It would be hard to find a better illustration of how many folk-songs are undoubtedly created. The story is simple and rather conventional; it includes situations and incidents that have often been sung in other familiar songs. So whenever the singer comes to one of these familiar incidents or situations, he falls back on the words of the other song. This is natural and probably almost unconscious. We do the same thing when we begin our fairy stories, as did our fathers before us, "Now once upon a time there lived a king who had two daughters." . . .

In the song below you will find stanzas lifted almost bodily from "The Boston Burglar," "The Rambling Boy," the old ballad of "The Maid Freed From the Gallows" (often called "The Hangman's Tree"), and from several others. Yet the result is far from being mere patchwork; it is an effective and on the whole a new story, pressing into service a number of old stanzas.

## THE GAME OF COON-CAN

### Text of W. F. B.

I went down to play a hand of coon-can;
I could not play my hand,
For I kept thinking of the girlie I loved
Ran away with another man.

Ran away with another man, poor boy,
Ran away with another man.
For I kept thinking of the girlie I loved
Ran away with another man.

I went down to the old depot
Just to watch the trains roll by;
I thought I saw the girlie I loved —
Hung down my head and cried.

[1] *Adventure*, December 20, 1925. For several years Mr. Gordon ably conducted in *Adventure* the department, "Old Songs that Men Have Sung." See also his interesting series of articles on "American Folk-Songs" in the *New York Times Magazine*, from January 2, 1927, on.

The night was dark and stormy
And it surely looked like rain;
I had not a friend in the whole wide world,
And nobody knew my name.

I caught a freight to Boston town —
I'd already searched the west —
For I was bent on finding
The girl that I loved best.

I landed in a fair little city
And there I found my pal;
I shot him once right through the heart
Just because he stole my gal.

The jury found me guilty,
And the Clerk he wrote it down;
The judge he passed the sentence on me,
And now I'm going to the penitentiary.

"Oh, say there, Mr. Hangman,
Won't you wait just a little while?
I think I see the girlie I loved,
And she's come for many a mile.

"Sweetheart, have you brought me silver?
Sweetheart, have you brought me gold?
Or have you come to see me hang
On yonder hangman's pole?"

"Yes, George, I've brought you silver,
And a stocking full of gold;
I could not bear to see you die
On yonder hangman's pole."

She took me in her parlor,
And she cooled me with her fan;
With the tears streaming down her cheeks she said,
"I love my highway-man."

The complicated and tangled history of the prolific "blues"[1]
shows all these possible lines of relationship and interrelation-
ship going on simultaneously. Tracing the genealogy of any

[1] See the chapter on "Blues" in Odum and Johnson, *Negro Workaday Songs*, and in Dorothy Scarborough, *On the Trail of Negro Folk-Songs*, Harvard University Press; W. C. Handy, *Blues, An Anthology*, A. C. Boni, New York, 1926; and Carl Sandburg, "Blues, Mellows, Ballets," in *The American Songbag*, pp. 223–256.

particular set of Blues is not unlike drawing a map of a spider-web — with a large question-mark in the centre.

A case in point has been recently described by Carl Sandburg,[1] who aptly terms it a vivid and hilarious minor incident in musical history.

Musical Chicago a few years ago looked with keen interest on a lawsuit. Two composers were each claiming to be the first and only music writer to score the Livery Stable Blues. On the witness stand the plaintiff testified that one evening, long before jazz had become either a vogue or an epidemic, his orchestra was playing in a cabaret, "and a lady dancer started doing some fancy steps, and I picks up a cornet and lets go a few pony neighs at her. The trombone come through with a few horse laughs. Then the banjos, cowbells, and sax puts in a lot of 'terpilations of their own. And that was the first time the Livery Stable Blues was played."

Thus musical history in America already has its traditions and controversies. The origin of jazz is still in a fog of wordy disputation. The years to come will see plenty of argument on other moot matters.

Much the same situation exists in regard to ballad tunes as in regard to ballad texts. Shifts and changes are constantly being made as the ballad progresses outward in space and forward in time. Tunes are interchanged, the exchange being made easy by the uniformity of the ballad measure. "Lady Isabel and the Elf Knight," for instance, has its own set of tunes. But the South Carolina B variant[2] borrowed, or rather adopted outright, the familiar and characteristic air of "Lord Lovel."

Individual composers have frequently based their music on strains or motifs from folk-music; and the reverse is equally true, the popular melodies of any day being folk-melodies in the making. It takes an effort to recall that "Annie Laurie," "Old Black Joe," "My Old Kentucky Home," and the like are artist-compositions.

Mr. Phillips Barry, who has devoted much study to ballad music, has analyzed in detail the effect of communal transmission on several ballad airs, most interestingly in connection with "Lord Randal."

[1] *The American Songbag*, Introd., p. vii.        [2] See below, p. 99.

Not only are at least ten sets [of airs] in existence [he finds], but from the same source as the melody to "Lord Randal" are descended the airs "Lochabar no More," "King James's March to Ireland," "Limerick's Lamentation," and "Reeve's Maggot."

Examples might be multiplied. Thus in the case of "Barbara Allen," it is certain that several distinct melodies have come down to us, resolved into sets by the re-creative force of oral tradition. The same may be proved for "The Golden Vanity." At some time in the nineteenth century a melody was sung to "Springfield Mountain," which now appears in a number of more or less diversified sets, each sung to a different version of the ballad. "Lord Randal," however, is in all probability unique as being the only old ballad which has retained its original melody.[1]

Mr. R. W. Gordon, who has been quoted previously,[2] describes the complicated relationship possible among contemporary song-variants as follows. [3]

Many of the minstrel songs — for example, songs sung on the stage by groups of white men made up to imitate negroes — were based upon or included folk material. And even before the period of the minstrel troupes, "Jump Jim Crow" was built up by "Daddy" Rice upon fragments that he heard sung by a wandering negro. The process still goes on: "Casey Jones," by Newton and Siebert, "It Ain't Gonna Rain No Mo'," by Wendell Hall, and the modern stage version of "Frankie and Johnny" are all readaptations of older material popular among the folk.

Still further complications are possible. Sometimes such made-over material gets back to the folk again and exerts an influence on true folk-song. This has happened in the case of "Casey Jones," mentioned above. Or a modern folk text and a modern "author" text, while having no direct relationship one with the other, may both be derived from a common original. It is never safe to be dogmatic in any given case unless all the evidence is in.

Similar testimony as to the situation among Negro secular folk-songs is given by Professor Newman I. White, who bases his opinion on a close study of 680 Negro secular songs.[4]

[1] Phillips Barry, "The Origin of Folk-Melodies," *J. A. F. L.*, vol. xxiii (1910), no. 90. "Lord Lovel" has also retained its original melody with exceptional uniformity.

[2] See above, pp. 48, 49.

[3] *Adventure*, January 10, 1925.

[4] Newman I. White, "The Derivation of Negro Secular Folk-Songs," paper read before the Popular Literature Section of the Modern Language Association at its 1927 meeting.

A "ballet" by a semi-literate negro or white man is sold at a fair or picnic and passes at once into oral tradition which sooner or later, by the immemorial process of repetition, amalgamation, addition, and garbling, absorbs it into the current of genuine folk-song.

Moreover . . . there is a problem of counter-influence from the folk-song. A ballet may simply be an elaboration of an older folk-song and may itself, after a little garbling, perhaps, become a part of other folk-songs. There are "ballets" of the Titanic, ballet and folk-song mixtures of the Titanic, and short folk-songs of the Titanic; but before there was a Titanic there was a folk-song about a forgotten Mississippi steam-boat, quoted by Mr. E. C. Perrow in the *Journal of American Folk-Lore* (1903, p. 123), which is sufficiently like the Titanic songs to show where the first Titanic song started.

Thus far, then, concerning the influence of oral tradition on contemporary songs. The value of such instances is the light they shed on what may have happened, and to a certain extent must have happened, to the traditional ballads before they were recorded in their present shape. As we have them, ballads go back through the fifteenth century; and there they stop.[1] There is nothing beyond except conjecture and theory.

And the crux of the theorizing, as has been stated, lies in communal composition. To restate it in question form: does communal transmission acting upon individual authorship adequately account for the traditional ballads, or is communal composition necessary as well to account for them?

As the general purpose of the sections on both communal composition and communal transmission is explanatory rather than argumentative, two answers may be quoted side by side. The first is that of Professor Hart.[2]

Professor Gummere's theory of ultimate communal origins is, then, a satisfactory explanation of the special characteristics of the popular ballads; so far as I know, it is the only explanation. And it has this wide significance: it shows that poetry was in its beginnings a natural function of the human mind, the creation of all the people for all the people, not made by the exceptional few for the exceptional few. Ballads are the one great and significant survival of this early

---

[1] The "Judas" ballad, however, exists in a thirteenth-century manuscript.
[2] Hart, Introd., p. 51.

universal poetry; of all poetry, therefore, they have the widest appeal, they are the most readily understood, the most easily appreciated.

The modified view is thus phrased by Professor Kittredge:[1]

The extant ballads of England and Scotland represent, in the main, the end of a process of which the beginning may not improbably be discovered in the period of communal composition. They were not themselves composed in this way, but were, in the first instance, the work of individual authors, at least in the great majority of cases.

It makes no difference whether a given ballad was in fact composed in the manner described [improvisation in the presence of a sympathetic company], or whether it was composed (or even written) in solitude, provided the author belonged to the folk, derived his material from popular sources, made his ballad under the inherited influence of the method described, and gave it to the folk as soon as he had made it, — and provided, moreover, the folk accepted the gift and subjected it to that course of oral tradition which, as we have seen, is essential to the production of a genuine ballad.[2]

The view of the present writer is similar, and may be stated as follows: there is strong presumptive evidence of communal composition in the case of a few of the simpler and earlier ballads; but the great majority of the traditional ballads are best accounted for on the theory of individual authorship in origin, plus a remolding and making-over through the objectifying and impersonalizing process of communal transmission.

[1] Kittredge, pp. xxiv, xxvii.

[2] Professor Gerould's opinion is to the same effect: "In whatever way the ballad originated, that is, it would be submitted to the same processes of remaking, once it came into popular favor. Provided it were in the suitable rhythm, a poem of sophisticated origin might well, it seems to me, have a long history as a ballad, alongside another poem that had sprung crude and simple from the excitement of a rural festival. Both narratives would pass under the same musical and poetic traditions.

"Grant this, and the old quarrel between communalists and individualists becomes superfluous. Why dispute about the origin of ballads if it is what happens to ballads in their diffusion that really matters?" (Gerould, pp. 22, 23.)

# V

## THE ROAD DOWNHILL

IT is generally held that oral tradition has tended to lower both the narrative effectiveness and the poetic quality of the ballads. Such phrases have been applied to it as "popular deterioration," "traditional debasement," and "the erosion of unretentive memories and inaccurate ears." T. F. Henderson, the Scottish foe of communalism whether in composition or in transmission, says unqualifiedly: "It tends to make the ballad 'popular,' in the sense of being mean and common and rude in style . . . for the simple reason that it has been gradually remoulded by the processes of instinctively stupid interference with the original text." [1]

Another student of balladry succinctly says: "After a painstaking study of the subject, I have yet to find a clear case where a ballad can be shown to have improved as a result of oral transmission, except in the way of becoming more lyrical." [2]

If one looks only at the present levels of oral tradition, such views are justified. But, in common with most things, oral tradition has, or at least once had, two sides. The other, constructive, side — oral tradition at its best and highest — must not be lost sight of. Without it, unless the theory of communal composition be assumed, there is no satisfactory way to account for the ballads at all. And the ballads are here to be accounted for, more than three hundred in the Scottish–English tradition, and more than five hundred in the Danish; a large body of narrative song with peculiar, individual qualities, essentially unlike any other body of verse in the world — except other ballads.

[1] Henderson, p. 71.
[2] John Robert Moore, "The Influence of Transmission on the English Ballads," *Modern Language Review*, xi, 400.

To say that oral tradition once had a constructive side means that there was a period in European civilization — probably during the fifteenth, sixteenth, and early seventeenth centuries — when oral tradition not only impersonalized, but also improved, that which was committed to it. And this, being interpreted in turn, means that there once were enough good Scottish and English heads unlettered in reading and writing to serve as a constructive medium for oral tradition to work through.

It is the penalty of oral tradition that it can exist only where literacy does not. The two vary inversely: as literacy waxes, oral tradition wanes; and as it wanes, it is automatically confined to lower and lower levels of talent and intelligence. In our day, owing to the universal spread of educational opportunity and cultural advantages, oral tradition has almost reached the vanishing-point in quantity, and has almost touched bottom in quality.[1]

The most obvious of its downhill effects is its tendency to change or corrupt unfamiliar or strange-sounding words in order to make them like, or identical with, more familiar words. This process, which is known as popular etymology, is but one phase of analogy, that great underlying principle of language which tends to sweep away all differences and to bring about general conformity of derivation, inflection, spelling, and pronunciation.

Popular etymology is one of the most prominent factors in oral tradition, and has worked strange and far-reaching results in the ballads. Within the brief time, for example, that Irwin Russell's "De Fust Banjo" has been subject to oral tradition, no fewer than five corruptions become evident on comparing the two versions given on pages 43 and 44: "Ham" has become "Sam"; "packet" (in the sense of steamboat) has become "package"; the phrase "f'om little E's to basses" has turned into "from

---

[1] Except among the Negroes, whose cultural status in certain sections still permits oral transmission to function vigorously and effectively, particularly as regards secular folk-songs and spirituals.

little east to graces," though it is given in its correct form in the final line of the same stanza; "playing" has become "saying," under the impression that "Nebber min' de wedder" was a remark instead of a tune; and the hyperbole "forty-lebben bands" has become "eleven banjos." This is a rather heavy load of errors to be laid upon one song in such a short time.

## I. Proper Names

Ballad proper names in especial, whether of persons or places, have undergone many curious changes. It would be interesting to trace the variations in the names of the heroes and heroines in the most widely spread ballads, but there is space for only a few.

"Lord Randal" is one of the most prolific of American ballad survivals, and has been recorded in many places in many variants. In these, from first to last, the hero's original name, Lord Randal, shows more than twenty changes, ranging as follows: Johnny Randolph, Johnny Ramsay, Johnny Reeler, Jimmy Randall, Jimmy Ransing, and Johnny Ramble — all clearly from the original Randal; also two wider variations, McDonald and Poor Anzo (both from South Carolina); and an interesting New England list: Lord Lantoun, Sweet William, Fair Elson, Sweet Nelson, Fair Nelson, Orlando, Fileander, Teronto, Tyrante, Tyranting, Terence; and two anonymous entitlements: "my own pretty boy" (Ireland and Massachusetts) and "my little rambling son" (colored, West Virginia).

The hero's name in another common ballad, "The Gypsy Laddie," ranges from Gypsy Geordie[1] to The Gyptian Laddie, Gypsen Davy or Davvy, Gypsy Davy, Black Jack Davy (Missouri), Black-boy Davy (North Carolina), and the Gypsy Daisy. In connection with a Gypsy Daisy variant from Massachusetts[2] a most interesting corruption in language has become transferred to the ballad-story itself, spoiling the plot and showing how unfortunate an effect a single verbal error can have.

---

[1] Child, No. 200, F1.
[2] Quoted by Phillips Barry, *J. A. F. L.*, vol. xviii, no. 70, p. 194.

The plot of "The Gypsy Laddie" turns on the heroine's leaving the attractions of home and family and following the gypsy for enchanted love.

In the variant referred to, the name "Daisy" seems to have worked its way from the refrain back into the text itself, and Daisy, being a girl's name, likewise carried its sex into the story, resulting in a sad mix-up of persons — for the heroine runs away with another girl instead of with a gypsy laddie.

The first three stanzas read:

> The Gypsy came from o'er the hills,
>   She sang so loud and boldly,
> She sang so loud it made the green woods ring —
>   They called her Gypsy Daisy.
>
> "Saddle up the dark bay horse,
>   The white one's not so speedy;
> I'll ride all night, I'll ride all day,
>   Till I overtake my Daisy.
>
> "Yes, I will leave my house and land,
>   Yes, I will leave my baby,
> Yes, I will leave my own true wedded lord,
>   To follow the Gypsy Daisy."

Sometimes the distortion in ballad names results in a humorous flavor that is as naïve as it is unintentional. In a Virginia variant of "Little Musgrave and Lady Barnard"[1] the leading actors are called Little Mosie Grove and Lord Burnett's Wife; in a British variant of "Barbara Allen," because of her hardness of heart toward her dying young man, Barbara is called Barbarous Ellen; and similarly, in a South Carolina variant of "Lord Thomas and Fair Annet," Lord Thomas, because of his inconstancy, is termed Low Thomas.

One of the most interesting of the ballad place-phrases, and one that has played a merry game of tag in oral tradition, occurs in the old Scottish ballad of "The Daemon Lover," or, as rationalized in recent survivals, "The House Carpenter."

[1] Louise Pound, *American Ballads and Songs*, Charles Scribner's Sons, 1922, p. 244, n. 15.

The lady in the case has finally been persuaded to forsake home
and children and to sail away with her (daemon) lover.  She
soon realizes her mistake and weeps bitterly.  Thereupon, in
Scott's version in *Minstrelsy of the Scottish Border*, the lover
promises:

> "O hauld your tongue of your weeping," says he,
>     "Of your weeping now let me be;
> I will shew you how the lilies grow
>     On the banks of Italy."

Various are the shapes this promise takes in American survivals.  A typical form is the following, from a West Virginia
variant:

> "If you will forsake your house-carpenter
>     And go along with me,
> I'll take you where the grass grows green
>     On the banks of Sweet Willie."

In other West Virginia variants the phrase runs, Sweet Italy,
sweet libertee, the sweet Morea; in North Carolina variants, the
Sweet Da Lee, Sweet Tennessee, Old Willie, Sweet Lillie, State
of Tennessee, salt-water sea;  in South Carolina, the cedar-see,
sweet re-lee;  in Pennsylvania, the banks of old Tennessee.  As
will be noticed, all of these variations keep both the rhythm of
the Scottish phrase (whatever that phrase itself may have been
originally) and the rime (or alliteration) of the final long *e*.

Another instance, with a similar metrical history, is the name
of the ship that sailed to the Lowlands in the ballad of "The
Sweet Trinity or the Golden Vanity."[1]  Both of these names
have a definite rhythm and both likewise rime on the long *e*
sound, a characteristic that they keep throughout the years.

The lilt of this ballad, even without a tune, is so attractive
that the opening stanzas of two American survivals are worth
quoting.

*From North Carolina*[2]

> There was a little ship in the South Amerikee,
> That went by the name of the Weeping Willow Tree,
> As she sailed upon the low-de-lands deep.

---

[1] Child, No. 286.          [2] Campbell and Sharp, No. 35, A.

There was another ship in the North Amerikee,
She went by the name of the Golden Silveree,
As she sailed upon the low-de-lands deep.

*From Kentucky*[1]

There was a little ship and she sailed upon the sea,
And she went by the name of The Mary Golden Tree;
As she sailed upon the lone and the lonesome low,
As she sailed upon the lonesome sea.

There was another little ship and she sailed upon the sea,
And she went by the name of the Turkish Robbery;
As she sailed upon the lone and the lonesome low,
As she sailed upon the lonesome sea.

Other variants for the names of the ships are The Green Willow Tree, The Golden Willow Tree, The Turkey Silvaree, and The French Gallilee.

## II. Individual Words

The variety of distortions in the case of unfamiliar individual words is almost unlimited. Nor is their humor unmixed with pathos, for they represent unconsciously heroic efforts on the part of successive folk-singers to reproduce words or phrases which carried no significance and conveyed no meaning to them. There is little difference between older and newer corruptions of this kind, except that the errors become both more numerous and more serious as recent times are approached. In the instances quoted below, the correct word or phrase is first given, followed by its corrupted form in italics.

*From the Older British Tradition*

"fashes" (that is, troubles, storms).

I wish the wind may never cease
Nor *fishes* in the flood.[2]

"But at Wentbridge"

But as he *went at a bridge*.[3]

---

[1] Wyman and Brockway, *Lonesome Tunes*, p. 72.
[2] "The Wife of Usher's Well," Child, No. 79, A.
[3] "A Gest of Robin Hood," Child, No. 117, st. 135.

[Correct reading uncertain]
Cocks are crowing *a merry mid-larf*.[1]

### From Recent British Tradition

"The laurel wore"
The third she was a virgin
And she the *lorrioware*.[2]

"It do rain in merry Lincoln"
Do rain, do rain, *American corn*.
Do rain both great and small.[3]

The puzzling "Mirry-land toune" of the first and thirteenth stanzas of Percy's version of the "Sir Hugh" ballad in the *Reliques*,[4] 1765, is almost certainly the same corruption, though more than two hundred and fifty years separate the recording of the two versions.

### From Recent American Tradition

"Adieu, adieu,"
*If you, if you*, to the ladies round [5]
*Bedew, bedew*, to the friends all round.[6]

Both corruptions preserve the assonance of the long *u*.

"Castle-gate . . . milk-white steed"
Lord Lovel he stood at his *cassy-gate*
A-combing his milk-white *speed*.[7]

"As it were to-day"
Lady Margaret was buried *on Wismer Day*.[8]

---

[1] "Sweet William's Ghost," Child, No. 77, B.
[2] S. Baring Gould and H. Fleetwood Sheppard, *Songs and Ballads of the West*, London, Methuen & Co., (third ed.), preface, p. ix.
[3] "Little Sir Hugh," Sharp, Introd., p.xx, and *English Folk Song: Some Conclusions* London, 1907, p. 95.
[4] Child, No. 155, B.
[5] A South Carolina variant of "Barbara Allen."
[6] A Virginia variant of the same.
[7] Quoted by Miss Mary Johnston from Virginia.
[8] West Virginia, "Fair Margaret and Sweet William," Cox, *A*.

"Bower door"
Down she fell from her *bowing door*.[1]
As she was sitting in her *dower room*.[2]

"Foot-page"
Little *foot-spade* (in several ballads)
Little *speed-foot* (once).[3]

"Ivory comb"
And down she threw her *high-row comb*.[4]

"Morocco shoes"
Fine *rockum shoes* and stockings.[5]

"Pen-knife"
Little *penny-knife* (a common corruption)

"Amain"
While all her friends cried out *amen*.[6]

"Tirl at the pin" (Scottish)
"Tinkle at the ring" (English).

The Scottish phrase, "to tirl at the pin," means to trill, or rattle, at that part of the door-fastening which lifts the latch. The pin was inside, fastened to a latch or leather point, the end of which was drawn through a small hole in the door to the outside. Compare the saying, "The latch-string hangs on the outside." During the daytime the pin was attached to a bar, or sneck, in such a way that, when the latch was pulled, the door was free to open. But at night the pin was disconnected from the door-fastening and hung loosely, so that, when the latch was pulled, the pin rattled.

In the corresponding English phrase, "to tinkle [or tingle] at the ring," the ring was the hammer of the door-knocker. In the case of tinkling, however, the ring was probably drawn up and

[1] West Virginia, "Fair Margaret and Sweet William," Cox, *D*.
[2] North Carolina, "Fair Margaret and Sweet William," Campbell and Sharp, *C*.
[3] North Carolina, "Little Musgrave and Lady Barnard," Campbell and Sharp, *G*.
[4] North Carolina, "Fair Margaret and Sweet William," Campbell and Sharp, *B*.
[5] North Carolina, "The Gypsy Laddie," Campbell and Sharp, *B*.
[6] West Virginia, "Barbara Allen," Cox, *A*.

down or struck against the projecting bow or rod of a door-handle (often wound with a spiral), an operation which, when vigorously performed, gave a risping or rasping sound.[1]

As fashions in door-fastenings changed, and pin and ring gave way to door-knob, knocker, and bell, the ballad phrases gave way, too, though in a different sense. Here are some of the end-products of these phrases in recent tradition, each line coming from a different ballad variant.

> She jingled at the ring
> And tingled low down at the ring
> And tingered low down at the ring
> Tingled at the wire
> So loudly she tingled and called
> Dingle at the ring
> He dingled so loud with the ring
> Dingled so low at the ring
> Dingled at the ring and it rung
> She knocked so loud upon the ring
> And he knocked at the ring
> So clearly he knocked at the ring
> He knocked till he made things ring
> Who knocks so loud and don't come in
> He knocked thereat, therein
> All jingling in the rings
> They rang their bells and dingled their rings
> { She went til she came to the gate, she tingled,
> { How boldly then she rang the bell
> How boldly she did ring the bell
> And then he rang the bell
> He knocked so loud on the door
> He knocks at the door, and picks up a pin.

### III. Organic Perversion

When the perversions of ballad language multiply beyond a certain point, the separate errors merge into a kind of pervasive degeneration that lowers the whole ballad to a most lamentable

[1] Definition from Kittredge, Glossary.

level — under dust to lie, sans song, sans singer, sans taste, sans everything.

Two examples will suffice, one from "Lord Thomas and Fair Annet" and the other from "Lord Randal," proud ballads both, with long and distinguished histories.

"Lord Thomas and Fair Annet" is contained in Percy's *Reliques* in two fine versions. It is one of the most beautiful of the ballads, and has had an extended career in oral tradition both in Great Britain and in America. In fact, with the exception of "Barbara Allen," it is the most widely found of all American ballad survivals. What seems to be its most corrupt variant was recorded in Pennsylvania about 1840.[1] In it Lord Thomas has sunk from being "a bold forester and a chaser of the king's deer" into "a bold biler, sir." Furthermore, fair Elendar is endowed not only with fairness but with wealth as well, so that Lord Thomas's mother has no reason for advising him to choose the Brown Girl,[2] thus breaking down the entire motivation of the plot.

> Lord Thomas was a bold biler, sir,
>   A biler, sir, was he;
> Fair Elendar being an accomplished young lady,
>   Lord Thomas loved her dearly, dearly,
>   Lord Thomas loved her dearly.
>
> "Go read me a riddle, dear mother," said he,
>   "Go riddle it all in wool;
> It's whether I'll make fair Elendar my bride,
>   Or bring me the brown girl home, home, home,
>   Or bring me the brown girl home.
>
> "Fair Elendar she has houses and lands,
>   The brown girl she has none;
> Before I'll be bothered with such a great peasant,
>   Go bring me the brown girl home, home, home,
>   Go bring me the brown girl home."

[1] Reported by Professor Albert H. Tolman, "Some Songs Traditional in the United States," *J. A. F. L.*, vol. xxix, no. 112.

[2] Professor Child earlier noted the same perversion in a copy taken from the singing of a Virginia nursemaid.

First prize, however, for organic perversion goes to a South Carolina variant of "Lord Randal."[1] Everything possible that oral tradition could inflict on any ballad has happened to it. The climax of bequests which the dying Lord Randal leaves to his relatives becomes a list of reasons why he left (in the sense of "forsook") his family. The "breely broth," wherewith his sweetheart has poisoned him in the traditional ballad story, becomes the dish which he would now like his mother to prepare for him before he "fails and lies down." In fact, Poor Anzo is so altogether changed from Lord Randal that it is surprising that his own mother knows him.

"What did you leave your dear father for, Anzo, my son,
What did you leave your dear father for, Anzo, my son?"
"He has six head of horses; make my bed soon;
I am sick in my heart, I should fail and lie down."

"What did you leave your dear mother for, Anzo, my son,
What did you leave your dear mother for, Anzo, my son?"
"She has plenty of kitchen furniture; make my bed soon;
I am sick in my heart, I should fail and lie down."

"What did you leave your dear sweetheart for, Anzo, my son,
What did you leave your dear sweetheart for, Anzo, my son?"
"Here is a red-hot iron will broil a bone brown,
She is the cause of my lying down."

"What will you have for supper, poor Anzo, my son,
What will you have for supper, poor Anzo, my son?"
"Make me a little breely broth soup,
For I'm sick in my heart, I should fail and lie down."

[1] See below, p. 103.

# VI

## THE BALLAD IN LITERATURE

ONE of the greatest pieces of creative research ever done in America is the monumental work of the late Professor Francis James Child of Harvard University, on the English and Scottish popular ballads. It appeared in five large volumes from 1882 to 1898, and is the authoritative resting-place of what has survived of the splendid body of English and Scottish ballads.

The surviving ballads are 305 in number and are known to enthusiasts almost as familiarly by their numbers in Child as by their titles. Practically all the ballads exist in many versions and variants. Child's collection was planned to include every extant version of every known ballad. For instance, nine versions of No. 4, "Lady Isabel and the Elf-Knight," are given; eighteen of No. 58, "Sir Patrick Spens"; and twenty-eight of No. 173, "Mary Hamilton."

Practically every ballad presents a problem in comparative literature. There is a striking similarity in tone, situation, and plot among the ballads, not only of England and Scotland, but of Denmark and of the other European countries as well. "The Hangman's Tree," for example, occurs in English, Scotch, German, Scandinavian, Sicilian, Finnish, Esthonian, and Russian, and has also been recorded in many American states. The Scotch ballad of "May Colvin" ("Lady Isabel and the Elf-Knight") is more widely spread still. Versions exist in English, Scotch, German, Danish, Norwegian, Swedish, Icelandic, Dutch, Low German, Spanish, Portuguese, Italian, French, Polish, Serbian, Bohemian, Wendish, and Magyar. It likewise is found in many places in the United States.

Ballads were extraordinarily numerous at one time. The fifteenth and early sixteenth centuries marked the high tide of balladry,[1] though ballads were not committed to writing till much later, only eleven ballads being preserved in manuscripts older than the seventeenth century. Both "Judas" and the "Hugh of Lincoln" ballad, however, go back to the thirteenth century, and from references in *Piers Plowman* it is clear that songs of Robin Hood and of Randolph, Earl of Chester, were current in 1350, the time of Chaucer's childhood. Some of the finest ballads are found only in the Percy manuscript, which was put together about 1650. Most of the 305 surviving ballads were taken down from oral tradition in Scotland within the last one hundred and seventy-five years.

There is no way of knowing how many ballads there were in all, originally, now lost forever. For it must be recalled that, like other forms of folk-lore, the ballads descended by oral tradition. They lived only as long as they were sung. Were it not for the incredible way that folk-lore has of spreading from country to country and keeping itself alive from generation to generation, it would be remarkable that so many ballads have survived.

It is interesting to speculate upon how many ballads were current in England and Scotland between 1500 and 1600. For example, there have come down to us no fewer than thirty-eight ballads dealing with Robin Hood alone. In these thirty-eight ballads there is a total of 7504 lines — enough to make a respectable book of two hundred and fifty pages, or, if fused into a connected whole by a single poet, enough to form an heroic epic.

Composed from before the time of Chaucer on, ballads played a familiar and important part in the life of the plain people.

---

[1] Ballad origins, of course, go much further back. A convenient summary is that of Professor Arthur Beatty in his article, "Ballad, Tale, and Tradition," *P. M. L. A.,* xxii, 98: "It would seem that the ballad, *as we have it,* is a distinct and individual phenomenon, appearing at a definite time in definite portions of Western Europe, through explicable causes, from 1100 to 1450, by borrowing from France in the first place, and then borrowing and reborrowing. But it does not appear everywhere in Western Europe: Iceland, Italy south of Piedmont, and portions of Spain have no ballads." Professor Beatty, in detail, dates the beginning of the ballad tradition in the Scandinavian countries about 1100 (very soon after that in England), in Germany about 1200, in Spain about 1400, in Italy about the same date, and in France between 1450 and 1500.

Shakspere, Beaumont and Fletcher, and the other Elizabethan dramatists quote numerous ballad snatches in their plays. Sir Philip Sidney, the Elizabethan ideal of chivalry, somewhat apologetically expresses the power of the native English ballads when he says in his *Defense of Poesie:* "Certainly I must confess my own barbarousness, I never heard the olde song of Percie and Douglas ["Chevy Chase"] that I found not my heart moved more than with a trumpet."

On the whole, however, the literary classes of Sidney's time paid little attention to the ballad, failing to realize its genuine poetic and social worth. Ballads were felt to be the exclusive property of the "spinsters and the knitters in the sun," and to be beneath the notice of the lords and ladies of England. If Shakspere's Juliet had been an English girl, the ballads she would have heard would have been sung by her old nurse, not by Romeo or the noble house of Capulet. Not until a century and a half after the death of Shakspere, after the Classic Age of Dryden, Pope, Addison, and Johnson had come and gone, did the ballad win its way into literary favor. Then it was taken up by the writers of the Romantic Period, who di.........
its artless melodies, simple diction, and impersonal directness a welcome contrast to the artificiality and sophistication of the Classic Age.

The ballad's enfranchisement took place in 1765, when Bishop Thomas Percy published his famous ballad collection, *Reliques of Ancient English Poetry*. The story of this work is one of the most interesting of the many hairbreadth escapes in literature. The precious folio manuscript which formed the basis of the *Reliques* was accidentally discovered by Percy under a bureau in the house of a friend, Sir Humphrey Pitt. A servant girl had put it there and was tearing off strips to light the fire with. A week or so later, and the whole manuscript would have gone up in smoke. Percy caught sight of it in time, and ballad history was made that day.

This invaluable manuscript is the source of some of the choicest ballad texts. It is in a hand of about 1650. Percy himself included forty-five ballads from it in the *Reliques*. After remaining in possession of the Percy family for a century, the whole manuscript was published in 1867–1868 through the combined efforts of Professor Child, Dr. Furnivall, and Professor Hales.

Launched under the impetus of a long and dignified, though slightly apologetic, preface, Percy's *Reliques* soon became nationally and even internationally known. Upon the younger enthusiasts of the dawning Romantic Movement, with only the polish, precision, purism, and perfection of the Classic Age as background, its influence was volcanic.

Scott's boyhood delight over discovering it called forth one of the most interesting passages in his autobiography:[1]

> I remember well the spot where I read these volumes for the first time. . . . The summer day sped onward so fast that notwithstanding the sharp appetite of thirteen, I forgot the hour of dinner, was sought for with anxiety, and was still found entranced in my intellectual banquet. . . . The first time, too, I could scrape a few shillings together, which were not common occurrences with me, I bought unto myself a copy of these beloved volumes; nor do I believe I ever read a book half so frequently, or with half the enthusiasm.

Scott's early enthusiasm for ballads never grew less. Almost fifty years later, within less than a year of his death, the picture is unchanged — this time drawn by Lockhart's pen under the date of July, 1831:

> It was again a darkish cloudy day, with some occasional mutterings of distant thunder, and perhaps the state of the atmosphere told upon Sir Walter's nerves; but I had never before seen him so sensitive as he was all the morning. . . . He . . . chanted, rather than repeated, in a sort of deep and glowing, though not distinct recitative, his first favorite among all the ballads ["The Battle of Otterburn"],—

> > It was about the Lammas tide,
> > When husbandmen do win their hay,
> > That the doughty Douglas bownde him to ride
> > To England to drive a prey, —

down to the closing stanzas, which again left him in tears —

> > "My wound is deep — I fain would sleep —
> > Take thou the vanguard of the three,

[1] Lockhart's *Life*, chap. 1.

And hide me beneath the bracken-bush,
That grows on yonder lily-lee."

Between these two scenes lies Scott's long and influential
career as ballad collector, poet, and novelist.  His *Minstrelsy
of the Scottish Border* (1802, 1803) and his Abbotsford Manuscripts were to Scotland what Percy's *Reliques* and folio manuscripts were to England.

Percy and Scott are household names in the ballad tradition,
but there were many others, both men and women, who between
1750 and 1850 contributed to the growing importance and influence of balladry — Ramsay, Herd, Ritson, Jamison, Mrs. Brown
of Falkland, Sharpe, Motherwell, Kinloch, Buchan, and Aytoun.
They all deserve to be gratefully remembered.

Not only in England, but in Germany as well, ballads began
to come in for a large share of attention from the Romantic
Movement.  Herder's *Volkslieder* (1778) aroused as much interest in Germany as Percy's *Reliques* had done in England.
Following folk models and using the familiar folk motif of the
return from the dead, Buerger produced in 1774 what is probably the most influential literary ballad ever written, "Lenore."
"Lenore" was translated by Scott under the title, "William and
Helen."  Its striking refrain runs:

Tramp! tramp! along the land they rode,
Splash! splash! along the sea,
The scourge is red, the spur drops blood,
The flashing pebbles flee.

The place that "Lenore" holds as the leading literary ballad
in the German Romantic Movement is, in the English tradition,
occupied by "William and Margaret."  This ballad is usually,
though mistakenly, attributed to David Mallet or Malloch
(1705-1767).  Like "Lenore," which it antedates by at least
fifty years, it is based on the "return from the dead" situation,
though it is the girl, not the man, who returns in the English
ballad.

Significant testimony to ballad influence on the contemporary poetry both of Germany and of England is given by Words-worth:[1]

I have already stated how Germany is indebted to this latter work [Percy's *Reliques*], and for our own country, its poetry has been ab-solutely redeemed by it. I do not think there is a writer in verse of the present day who would not be proud to acknowledge his obliga-tions to the *Reliques*. I know that it is so with my friends; and for myself, I am happy in this occasion to make a public avowal of my own.

Thus it was that the popular ballad gained entrance into Euro-pean literature. Launched by Percy's *Reliques*, Scott's *Minstrelsy of the Scottish Border*, Mallet's "William and Margaret," and Buerger's "Lenore," it grew in literary favor until it spread over Germany, England, and Scotland. The Romantic Movement found two of the leading traits of Romanticism exemplified in the ballad: the return to the human heart, and interest in primi-tive poetry and mediaeval literature as suggestive of an heroic age. The Romantic poets first admired and then imitated the ballad fashion of telling a story. Wordsworth shows strong ballad influence in "Lucy Gray" and other poems. Keats's beautiful "La Belle Dame sans Merci" shows it more clearly still. But it was reserved for Coleridge to produce in "The Ancient Mariner" the greatest literary ballad of all time. While not so great a poet as either Wordsworth, Keats, or Coleridge, Scott was temperamentally much closer to the ballad tradi-tion, and tried his hand successfully many times on the type. Familiar examples are "Lochinvar," "Allan-A-Dale," "Proud Maisie," and "Jock o' Haseldean." His work approximates the popular ballad as closely as it is humanly possible for a conscious literary artist to come to a genuine folk type. His "Kinmont Willie" is the one ewe-lamb of individual artistry that can mingle undetected with the communal flock.

Many later poets have used the ballad stanza, and with vary-ing success have imitated the ballad technique. Tennyson's lyric craftsmanship was not suited to the ballad, and "Lady

[1] Wordsworth, "Essay, Supplementary to the Preface," 1815.

Clare," "The Revenge," and "The Charge of the Light Brigade" are the nearest approach he either could or would make. It is interesting to recall that Rossetti, like Scott, whom he resembled in little else, fell under the sway of the *Reliques* as a boy, translated Buerger's "Lenore," and wrote three notable literary ballads, "The Blessed Damozel," "Sister Helen," and "Troy Town." Likewise the "Ballad of Reading Gaol" is Oscar Wilde's best-known poem.

Leading American ballads, by the older group of poets, are Longfellow's "Wreck of the Hesperus" and "Skeleton in Armor," Lanier's "Revenge of Hamish," and Whittier's "Skipper Ireson's Ride." The best examples among the more recent writers on both sides of the Atlantic are John Davidson's "A Ballad of Hell," Kipling's "Danny Deever" and "The Ballad of Fultah Fisher's Boarding House," Yeats's "Father Gilligan," Masefield's "Yarn of the Loch Achray," "Hounds of Hell," and "Cap on Head," Alfred Noyes's "The Highwayman," and Amy Lowell's "Four Sides to a House."

To sum up, such has been the literary history of the ballad. Reaching its climax in numbers and effectiveness during the late fourteenth, fifteenth, and early sixteenth centuries, it gradually declined as English life increased in political, social, and religious complexity, in class consciousness, in education, and in general sophistication.

Alongside the genuine old ballads of oral tradition, and profiting by their favor, there later appeared in increasing numbers the cheap contemporary stall and broadside ballads. These were sometimes built up from genuine old fragments and situations, but were oftener thrown together to journalize the leading crime sensation or thrill in the news of the day. Thus closed the creative age of the English ballad tradition. Too many people had learned to read and write for oral transmission to continue to transmit effectively.

The next step was the discovery of the ballad as a type and its adoption into favor in the highest literary circles. During the hundred years before and after 1800, the European Romantic

Movement accorded international recognition to the ballad, and it was widely imitated by conscious literary artists. Antiquarian interest and a zeal for ballad collecting succeeded in recovering a great many of the traditional ballad texts and tunes, culminating in Child's authoritative list of 305 English and Scottish ballads preserved in many versions and variants, and in Grundvig's great collection in Denmark.

# VII

# THE BALLAD IN AMERICA

THE United States occupies a somewhat peculiar position as regards folk-lore, in that it is a recent offshoot of an older civilization. It was colonized and fought over by three European nations, England finally emerging victorious in war and predominant in national and racial influences. We have to jog our memories to recall that the Indians are the only native Americans, and that we Caucasians are interlopers of yesterday. Likewise the Negro, coming from another continent, or rather brought against his will, has contributed his own racial background of superstitions, customs, beliefs, tales, songs, and language. Indian, West European, Negro — we have them all, in both race and lore.

Our folk-lore is predominantly English, as are our language and literature. It is not surprising, therefore, to find that many of the traditional English and Scottish ballads crossed the Atlantic with the settlers and took root on American soil. Here they have remained, subject to the same chances and changes of oral tradition in their new home that their English and Scottish analogues were (and are) subject to in theirs.

Most of our ballads probably came over in the seventeenth, eighteenth, and early nineteenth centuries. Not only the colonists and the later English, Scotch, and Scotch-Irish settlers and emigrants, but also returned travellers, visitors, and sailors were the means of transmitting ballads to American shores.

Thus up and down the Atlantic seaboard, from Nova Scotia to Georgia, the folk-songs of Great Britain were transplanted in a new environment and under strange conditions.

Most of the ballads were at first confined to the coast districts. As the tide of population flowed farther and farther westward, however, the ballads went too, though in decreasing proportion.

The situation in Nebraska, for instance, is probably typical. Of the nine variants of the seven ballads found there, three came from Missouri, two from Indiana, two from Illinois, one from Virginia, and one from Ohio.[1]

On the way westward, the great Appalachian highlands were gradually and sparsely settled. This region to-day contains the richest store of ballads, in both numbers and purity, to be found in America. For here the conditions for ballad preservation were (and are) ideal. Almost every characteristic of place and people seemed made to order for that purpose. Racial purity and integrity; intense conservatism of language, customs, and social background; comparative isolation — in many communities complete isolation — from the chaotic impact of modern civilization; primitive conditions of life, simple habits of thought, and naïve standards of taste — all these have persisted in combination, forming a social fabric wonderfully tenacious of the lore of the past.

It is not surprising, therefore, to find that the highlands of North Carolina, Virginia, West Virginia, and Kentucky have yielded gratifying results to the collector of ballads. About ten years ago, for example, Mr. Cecil Sharp, the distinguished English authority on folk-songs, came to America and, accompanied by Mrs. Olive Dame Campbell of Asheville, North Carolina, made a nine weeks' trip through the mountains of North Carolina and Kentucky in search of material. They discovered and recorded the remarkable total of 122 songs and ballads and 323 tunes. Of these, no fewer than 37 are traditional ballads listed by Child.[2]

What Mr. Sharp has to say about conditions surrounding American balladry is of peculiar value because he is an acknowledged authority in the English field. He thus has a unique background for drawing comparisons between the British and the American folk-song traditions.

---

[1] See Miss Pound's article, "Traditional Ballads in Nebraska," *J. A. F. L.*, xxvi, 351–366. It is probable, also, that the Indiana and Illinois variants came eventually from the Atlantic seaboard.

[2] These valuable findings, including both texts and melodies, have been published with the title, *English Folk Songs from the Southern Appalachians*. Putnam's, 1917.

Of his experiences in the North Carolina mountains he writes: [1]

The present inhabitants of the Laurel Country are the direct descendants of the original settlers who were emigrants from England and, I suspect, the lowlands of Scotland. I was able to ascertain with some degree of certainty that the settlement of this particular section began about three or four generations ago, *i.e.*, in the latter part of the eighteenth century or early years of the nineteenth. How many years prior to this the original emigration from England had taken place, I am unable to say; but it is fairly safe, I think, to conclude that the present-day residents of this section of the mountains are the descendants of those who left the shores of Britain some time in the eighteenth century.

The region is from its inaccessibility a very secluded one. There are but few roads — most of them little better than mountain tracks — and practically no railroads. Indeed, so remote and shut off from outside influence were, until quite recently, these sequestered mountain valleys that the inhabitants have for a hundred years or more been completely isolated and cut off from all traffic with the rest of the world. Their speech is English, not American, and, from the number of expressions they use which have long been obsolete elsewhere, and the old-fashioned way in which they pronounce many of their words, it is clear that they are talking the language of a past day, though exactly of what period I am not competent to decide. One peculiarity is perhaps worth noting, namely, the pronunciation of the impersonal pronoun with an aspirate — "hit" — a practice that seems to be universal. . . .

My sole purpose in visiting this country was to collect the traditional songs and ballads which I had heard from Mrs. Campbell, and knew from other sources, were still being sung there. I naturally expected to find conditions very similar to those which I encountered in England when engaged on the same quest. But of this I was soon to be agreeably disillusioned. Instead, for instance, of having to confine my attention to the aged, as in England, where no one under the age of seventy ordinarily possesses the folk-song tradition, I discovered that I could get what I wanted from pretty nearly everyone I met, young and old. In fact, I found myself for the first time in my life in a community in which singing was as common and almost as universal a practice as speaking. . . .

The mountain singers sing in very much the same way as English folk-singers, in the same straightforward, direct manner, without any conscious effort at expression, and with the even tone and clarity of enunciation with which all folk-song collectors are familiar. Perhaps, however, they are less un-self-conscious and sing rather more freely

---

[1] Campbell and Sharp, Introd., pp. iv ff.

and with somewhat less restraint than the English peasant; I certainly never saw any one of them close the eyes when he sang, nor assume that rigid, passive expression to which collectors in England have so often called attention.

The wonderful charm, fascinating and well-nigh magical, which the folk-singer produces upon those who are fortunate enough to hear him is to be attributed very largely to his method of singing, and this, it should be understood, is quite as traditional as the song itself. The genuine folk-singer is never conscious of his audience — indeed, as often as not, he has none — and he never, therefore, strives after effect nor endeavors in this or in any other way to attract the attention, much less the admiration, of his hearers. So far as I have been able to comprehend his mental attitude, I gather that, when singing a ballad, for instance, he is merely relating a story in a peculiarly effective way which he has learned from his elders, his conscious attention being wholly concentrated upon what he is singing and not upon the effect which he himself is producing. This is more true, perhaps, of the English than of the American singers, some of whom I found were able mentally to separate the tune from the text — which English singers can rarely do — and even in some cases to discuss the musical points of the former with considerable intelligence. . . .

None of the singers whom I visited possessed any printed song-sheets but some of them produced written copies, usually made by children, which they called "ballets," a term which the English singer reserves for the printed broadside.

Ever since the publication of Child's collection, the American Folk-Lore Society, the separate state folk-lore societies, and various other organizations and persons have been collecting ballads, so that a large and steadily growing number of American survivals has been recorded and listed. Mr. Sharp's American experiences have been quoted in detail because of his English background.[1]

In the United States, the New England states in particular have been carefully worked, and on last accounts had yielded 25 ballads in many different variants and tunes.[2] The South, however, because of the richness of the Southern Appalachians

---

[1] For his views on the English field, see his *English Folk-Song: Some Conclusions*, Novello and Co., London, 1907.

[2] See the various articles of Mr. Phillips Barry of Cambridge, Mass., in the *J. A. F. L.*

in folk-song, has yielded better returns than any other section in America. Its present total is 69.

With all possible sources of information utilized, the total composite list of traditional ballads recovered in the United States as a whole now stands at 92.

The total for Canada seems to be 15, and for America, 95.

The details of the way these lists were arrived at are given in the Appendix.

According to available evidence, it seems that the number of ballads surviving in England is 85.[1] Mr. Sharp's opinion after his visit to our shores would seem to be that balladry is not only more vigorous, but destined to survive longer, in this country than in England.

What the future may bring forth in the way of increasing our stock of surviving ballads is uncertain, but it seems unlikely that existing totals will be greatly added to, except in the discovery of additional variants and tunes. Mr. Sharp seems inclined to this view when he says of his North Carolina investigations:[2]

Indeed, when we consider into what a very small portion of the field we have as yet carried our investigations, the magnitude of the task before us seems overwhelming. But this may not in reality be so, for it may not, after all, be necessary to pursue our researches throughout the whole of the area with the same care that we have already given, say, to the Laurel Country. For folk-singing in the mountains is so live an art and so general a practice that in all probability by the time we have collected a certain number of songs—not necessarily a very great number — we shall find that we have exhausted the field.

It would seem probable that future progress in the study of American balladry will be in the direction of recovering and comparing variant texts and tunes of existing ballads, rather than in the discovery of hitherto unrecorded American ballads. The wideness of a ballad's geographical occurrence, its present "popularity," so to speak, is almost as important as the fact that it has survived at all. For example, the five ballads most generally distributed in New England are "The Elfin Knight," "Lady

[1] Smith, p. 111.  [2] Campbell and Sharp, Introd., p. xxii.

Isabel and the Elf Knight," "Lord Randal," "Bonny Barbara
Allen," and "The Gypsie Laddie"; those found most widely
in the South are "Lady Isabel and the Elf Knight," "Lord
Thomas and Fair Elinor," "Lord Lovel," "Bonny Barbara
Allen," and "The Maid Freed from the Gallows." Of all American survivals, "Bonny Barbara Allen" easily leads both in the
number of variants and in the number of tunes.

Such features of the American ballad tradition would seem
as significant as the fact that an interesting group of five Robin
Hood ballads [1] has as yet been discovered only in Virginia of
all the American states.

To sum up, at the present time ballad tradition and ballad
influence are manifesting themselves in three ways: first, the
perseverance of popular ballads in contemporary oral tradition,
approximately one third of the original 305 being still sung
in England and in America; [2] second, contemporary composition
of ballads in places and under conditions resembling those of
earlier times, the products of which are exceedingly interesting
but greatly inferior in quality to the traditional ballads; third,
the imitation of popular ballads by individual poets and singers.

At the close of his article on balladry, which has already been
quoted from, [3] Professor Gerould has an excellent summary of
the ballad situation as it exists in America at present:

I suppose that any self-centered community [he says] that sings
at its work and its play is capable of producing authentic ballads.
I see no reason to think, however, that now or at any future time
there can exist the peculiar conditions that gave rise to the majority
of the ballads in the great collections of Child and Grundtvig. Those
conditions have gone, and the traditions they sustained have nearly
disappeared. Such slips from the original stock as were transplanted
to the New World, here to flourish less beautifully, are now fast de-
caying. There is no use in trying to stay the process, I am afraid,
for an essential virtue of folk-song must be its unconsciousness. All

---

[1] "Robin Hood and Guy of Gisborne," "Robin Hood's Death," "Robin Hood and
Little John," "Robin Hood and the Tanner," "Robin Hood Rescuing Will Stutley."

[2] Allowing for the existence of nine or ten ballads in oral tradition which as yet are
undiscovered and unrecorded.

[3] "The Making of Ballads," *Mod. Phil.*, vol. xxi. See above, pages 39 and 53, note 2.

we can do is to keep the old ballads in remembrance as long as possible, and to gather up before it perishes the precious evidence they present as to the times when ballad-making was a natural outlet for the feelings and fancies of rural folk. There were poets and composers in those days to whom art was not a trade. Some of them were gifted, I take it, and very many of them able to do no more than lisp in numbers; but all alike helped to form and to preserve a tradition of song that in retrospect must be judged one of the greater glories of our race.

# VIII

# FIVE HUNDRED YEARS OF "THE MAID FREED FROM THE GALLOWS"

"THE Maid Freed from the Gallows" — or "The Hangman's Tree," as it is known in America — is one of the oldest, most typical, and most interesting of the ballads. There are thirteen versions in Child,[1] and analogues exist in large numbers in Sicilian, Spanish, Faroese, Icelandic, Swedish, Danish, German, Esthonian, Wendish, Russian, Little-Russian, and Slovenian, as well as in Scottish and English. It has wide currency in America, and has been reported from practically every state

[1] F. J. Child, *The English and Scottish Popular Ballads*, II, 346–355. Child's thirteen versions are derived as follows:

A. Percy: communicated April 7, 1770.

B. Motherwell.

C. *Notes and Queries*, 1883; communicated 50 or 60 years previously.

D. Skene MSS, taken down in North or Northeast Scotland, 1802, 1803.

E. Buchan's MSS.

F. *Notes and Queries*, 1882, "as sung 40 years ago."

G. *Notes and Queries*, 1882.

Ha. Baring-Gould's Appendix to Henderson's notes on the *Folk-Lore of the Northern Countries of England and the Border*, 1866; a Yorkshire story called "The Golden Ball," mixing prose narrative and verse.

Hb. A Newcastle-on-Tyne story of a golden ball; prose up to execution, then verse.

Hc. A Cornish story of mixed prose and verse.

I. Scotch Ballads, material for Border Minstrelsy.

J. Communicated by Dr. George B. Hill, May 10, 1890, as learned forty years before from a schoolfellow who came from the north of Somersetshire and sang it in the dialect of that region.

K. "The Prickly Bush," a recent English version from Somersetshire, containing a fourth refrain stanza:

> Oh, the prickly bush, the prickly bush,
>   It pricked my heart full sore;
> If ever I get out of the prickly bush,
>   I'll never get in any more.

L. A fragment.

M. A North Carolina version described as "an old English song brought over to Virginia before the Revolution."

where ballads have been collected. It is especially common in the South, and is easily the favorite of all the traditional ballads among the Negroes.

So manifold are the changes it has undergone throughout its far-flung career in oral tradition that its history is particularly interesting, and is worth being set forth in some detail.

The situation that the ballad story is based on is clear even from a hurried reading (or hearing). The girl has been condemned to die, presumably for the loss (or theft) of a golden (or silver) ball or comb or key. In the foreign forms of the ballad, the victim has usually fallen into the hands of corsairs or pirates, who demand ransom; but none of the English or American versions account for the situation in this way. As the condemned girl stands with the rope around her neck, she sees a cloud of dust in the distance and hopes it is one of her relatives coming to her rescue. Her whole family connection arrives, one after the other, but none can or will help her till the climax is reached and her truelove comes and saves her. In a few versions the situation is reversed. It is the man who stands condemned and his sweetheart who rescues him.

A version quoted by Professor Kittredge and described as having been brought over to Virginia before the revolution, has rare simplicity and impressiveness of language, with a tune admirably matching these qualities.

### THE MAID FREED FROM THE GALLOWS

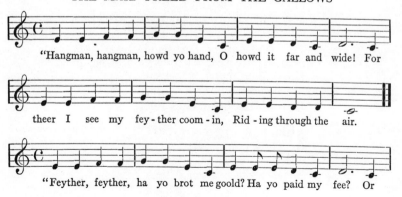

"Hangman, hangman, howd yo hand, O howd it far and wide! For theer I see my fey-ther coom-in, Rid-ing through the air.

"Feyther, feyther, ha yo brot me goold? Ha yo paid my fee? Or

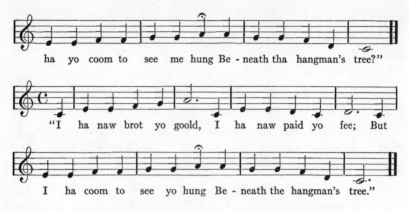

ha yo coom to see me hung Be - neath tha hangman's tree?"

"I ha naw brot yo goold, I ha naw paid yo fee; But

I ha coom to see yo hung Be - neath the hangman's tree."

> "Hangman, hangman, howd yo hand,
> O howd it far and wide!
> For theer I see my feyther coomin,
> Riding through the air.

> "Feyther, feyther, ha yo brot me goold?
> Ha yo paid my fee?
> Or ha yo coom to see me hung
> Beneath tha hangman's tree?"

> "I ha naw brot yo goold,
> I ha naw paid yo fee;
> But I ha coom to see yo hung
> Beneath the hangman's tree."

[And so on for mother, sister, and so forth, through the climax of relatives, till the truelove or sweetheart comes]:

> "Hangman, hangman, howd yo hand,
> O howd it wide and far!
> For theer I see my sweetheart coomin,
> Riding through the air.

> "Sweetheart, sweetheart, ha yo brot me goold?
> Ha yo paid my fee?
> Or ha yo coom to see me hung
> Beneath tha hangman's tree?"

> "O I ha brot yo goold,
> And I ha paid yo fee,
> And I ha coom to take yo froom
> Beneath tha hangman's tree."

In the British version of practically the same age, communicated to Bishop Percy in 1770 (Child *A*), the judge is addressed directly, instead of the hangman, and the relatives appear to be particularly hardhearted.

> "O good Lord Judge, and sweet Lord Judge,
>     Peace for a little while!
> Methinks I see my own father,
>     Come riding by the stile.
>
> "Oh father, oh father, a little of your gold,
>     And likewise of your fee!
> To keep my body from yonder grave,
>     And my neck from the gallows-tree."
>
> "None of my gold now shall you have,
>     Nor likewise of my fee;
> For I am come to see you hanged,
>     And hanged you shall be."

Throughout its long career, this ballad has held its original form surprisingly well. Of course its framework, of three stanzas and repeat, is very simple and peculiarly well suited both to being easily remembered and to group singing. It is a striking instance of incremental repetition, in which the same words are repeated in a set of stanzas, with just enough change or addition to advance the story one step. This gives the familiar "leaping and lingering" effect, as it has been called by Professor Gummere. As soon as the first three stanzas have been heard, the ballad audience can join in and sing the rest of it *ad infinitum*, till all the heroine's hardhearted relatives have arrived, one after the other, followed by the truelove by way of climax.

But while the structure of "The Maid Freed from the Gallows" has not changed, its tone and setting have. "Other times, other manners" applies with peculiar force to ballads. From them one can readily learn the company they have kept.

Contemporary English versions bear the title of "The Prickly Bush," or "The Briery Bush," from a fourth stanza, which is added to and repeated with the original framework of three. In Sharp's *One Hundred English Folksongs* this additional refrain stanza reads:

"O the briery bush,
    That pricks my heart so sore;
If I once get out of the briery bush
    I 'll never get in any more.

This additional lament of the girl adds a lighter lyrical touch, which is more characteristic of folk-songs than of ballads.

A Kentucky version from Wyman and Brockway's *Lonesome Tunes* opens thus:

"Hangman, hangman, slack up your rope,
    O slack it for a while,
I looked over yonder and I see Paw coming,
    He's walked for many a long mile."

"Say Paw, say Paw, have you brung me any gold,
    Any gold for to pay my fine?"
"No sir, no sir, I've brung you no gold,
    No gold for to pay your fine,
But I'm just come to see you hanged,
    Hanged on the gallows line."

"Oh you won't love and it's hard to be beloved,
    And it's hard to make up your time,
You have broke the heart of many a true love,
    True love, but you won't break mine."

And this from a North Carolina mountaineer's variant:[1]

"Hold up your hand, O Joshuay," she cried,
    "Wait a little while and see;
I think I hear my own father dear
    Come a-rambling over the sea."

Each of these versions bears its autobiography on its face, and might say with that other ancient wanderer, Ulysses, "I am part of all that I have met." Reading between the lines, one could almost reconstruct the different backgrounds and social environments in which they received their present form. It is this fact which makes the study of oral tradition so fascinating and at the same time so difficult.

As was said earlier, sometimes the rôles of maid and truelove

---

[1] Campbell and Sharp, p. 106, *A* and *B*. Compare Cox, p. 118.

are interchanged, and it is the girl who rescues the man. This is the case in an Australian version, called "Johnnie Dear," which, however, was learned in this country.[1] It closes:

"Hold up your head, dear Johnnie!
  Hold it up for a while!
I think I see your sweetheart a-coming,
  Walking many a mile."

"Have you brought me gold, dear sweetheart?
  Have you brought me a fee?
Or have you come for to see me hung
  Upon this Tyburn tree?"

"I have brought you gold, dear Johnnie,
  I have brought you a fee,
And I've come for to take you home
  Away from this Tyburn tree!"

### AMONG THE NEGROES

"The Hangman's Tree" is a favorite among the Negroes,[2] probably because of its marked dramatic quality and because its repetitive framework of stanzas is so easily remembered. In fact, the structure of many of the Negro revival hymns and spirituals is strikingly like that of this ballad. In them, as in it, the unit of repetition is easily grasped, and the rest of the song is swung around the pivotal words contributed by different singers. Take, for instance, these typical Negro hymns:

### SAVE ME, LORD SAVE ME

1. I called to my father,
     My father hearkened to me.
   And the last word I heard him say
     Was, save me, Lord, save me.

2. I called to my mother, *etc.*

  3 and following. I called to my sister, brother, preacher, leader, children, *etc.*

---

[1] Reported by R. W. Gordon in *Adventure*, July 23, 1926, pp. 189, 190.
[2] Miss Dorothy Scarborough describes and quotes several Negro variants in *On the Trail of Negro Folk-Songs*, Harvard University Press, 1925, pp. 35–43, 283, 284.

### Going to Shout all over God's Heaven

1. I got a robe, you got a robe,
   All God's chillun got a robe;
   When I get to Heaven, going to put on my robe,
   Goin' to shout all over God's Heav'n.

2. I got a crown, etc.

3 and following. I got a shoes, a harp, a song, etc.

### He'd be There [1]

1. "I think I heard Brother Johnson say
   He'd be there."
   
   [All shout]: "Brother Johnson!"
   
   "I think I heard Brother Johnson say
   He'd be there."
   
   [All shout]: "Brother Johnson!"
   
   "I think I heard Brother Johnson say
   He'd be there."
   
   [All shout]: "Brother Johnson!"

2. "I think I heard Sister Barbridge say," etc.

3 and following. "I think I heard" the names of as many of the congregation as there are time and desire to include.

### Resurrection of Christ

1. Go and tell my disciples,
   Go and tell my disciples,
   Go and tell my disciples,
   Jesus is risen from the dead.

2. Go and tell Sister Mary and Martha, etc.

3 and following. Go and tell poor sinking Peter, the Roman Pilate, poor doubting Thomas, the weeping mourners, etc.

One of the most interesting of the Negro variants of "The Hangman's Tree" is the South Carolina one given in full below.[2] It refers to the scarlet tree instead of the gallows-tree, and specifically names a golden ball as the cause of the impending tragedy.

[1] Submitted by Mr. S. B. Love, of Richmond, Va.
[2] Pages 144–147.

"Hangman, hangman, hold your hand
  A little longer still;
I think I see my father coming
  And he will set me free.

"Oh father, father, have you brought
  My golden ball and come to set me free?
Or have you come to see me hung
  Upon the Scarlet Tree?"

"I have not brought your golden ball,
  Or come to set you free;
But I have come to see you hung
  Upon the Scarlet Tree."

A Negro version from Virginia opens:[1]

"O hangman, hold your holts, I pray,
  O hold your holts awhile,
I think I see my grandmother
  A-coming down the road."

And this, also, is from a Negro Virginia version:[2]

"O hangerman, hangerman, slack on your rope,
  And wait a little while,
I think, I see my father a-coming
  And he's traveled for many a long mile."

From St. Helena Island,[3] just off the coast of South Carolina, a complete Gullah [4] Negro variant was recently recorded.[5]  It follows the usual triad pattern.  The air and the first three stanzas are as follows:

[1] Smith, p. 118.

[2] *Ibid.*, p. 119.

[3] St. Helena has a population of approximately 6000 Negroes and 60 white people. The Penn School, founded during the War between the States, was the first school for Negroes in the South supported by Northern funds. It has been brought to a high degree of efficiency by Miss Rossa B. Cooley, who went there in 1903. It dominates the island settlement, and has had a tremendous influence upon it — so much so that the St. Helena Negroes are considerably above their racial average in most ways.

[4] For a discussion of the origin, dialect, *etc.*, of the Gullah Negroes, see the writer's monograph, "Gullah," *Bulletin of the University of South Carolina*, November, 1926.

[5] Elsie Clews Parsons, "Folk-Lore of the Sea Islands, South Carolina," *Memoirs American Folk-Lore Society*, xvi (1923), 189, 190.

### THE HANGMAN'S TREE

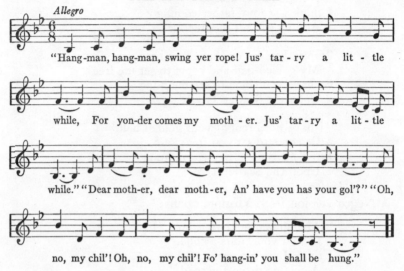

"Hang-man, hang-man, swing yer rope! Jus' tar-ry a lit-tle while, For yon-der comes my moth-er. Jus' tar-ry a lit-tle while." "Dear moth-er, dear moth-er, An' have you has your gol'?" "Oh, no, my chil'! Oh, no, my chil'! Fo' hang-in' you shall be hung."

In regard to the dramatic quality of "The Hangman's Tree" and the ballads in general, it was earlier remarked how naturally they could be turned into little dramatic scenes or plays that would almost act themselves.[1] There are three instances on record, all from Virginia, of exactly this having taken place among the Negroes in connection with "The Hangman's Tree." The most interesting account is that given by an eye-witness in a letter written in 1913.[2]

It was a long time ago — probably twenty-five years — at the colored schoolhouse, as a part of the closing exercises of the school. We young people always attended these exercises if possible, because we were sure of being highly entertained. This particular play I remember better than any other I ever saw there because we thought it so very funny, though plainly intended to be so very sad. They had on the stage a rather crude representation of the upper part of a scaffold. A rope the size of a man's wrist was thrown over the cross-beam, an end being tied around the neck of a most dejected-looking girl, and the other end held in the hand of a middle-aged man of sternest aspect. She alone did any singing. The apparently endless procession of relatives recited their parts very glibly, until at last, when her "truelove" arrived, he sang his part, and then the lovers

---

[1] See above, p. 10.          [2] Smith, p. 119.

ended the play with a joyous duet. I did not know then that it was a ballad.

With this incident may be compared the statement of the lady who communicated a West Virginia variant:[1] "When I was a little girl I used to play it."

A strange mixture of song and story, akin to the *cante-fable* form, has been recorded from the Negro lore of Jamaica. One version motivates the situation through the plotting of an enraged stepmother:[2]

There was a man have two daughter. One of the daughter belongs to the wife an' one belongs to the man. An' the wife no love for the man daughter, so they drive her away.

An' she got a sitivation at ten shillings a week, an' the work is to look after two horses an' to cut dry grass for them.

An' every night she put two bundles of dry grass in the 'table.

An' the mother was very grudgeful of the sitivation that she got.

An' one night she carry her own daughter to the pastur' an' they cut two bundles of green grass. An' they go secretly to the horse manger an' take out the dry grass an' put the green grass in its place.

So the horse eat it, and in the morning they died.

An' the master of that horse is a sailor.

The sailor took the gal who caring the horse to hang her.

An' when he get to the 'pot a place to hang her, he take this song:

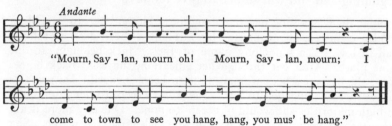

"Mourn, Say - lan, mourn oh! Mourn, Say - lan, mourn; I come to town to see you hang, hang, you mus' be hang."

An' the gal cry to her sister an' brother an' lover, an' they give her answer:

"Sis-ter, you bring me some sil-ver?" "No, my child, I bring you none."

---

[1] Cox, p. 115.

[2] Its local name is "Saylan." See Walter Jekyll, *Jamaican Song and Story*, David Nutt, London, 1907, pp. 58 ff. Another version is given by Miss Martha W. Beckwith in "The English Ballad in Jamaica," *P. M. L. A.*, vol. xxxix, no. 2, pp. 475, 476.

"Brother, you bring me some gold?" "No, my child,  I  bring  you  none."

"Lov-er, you bring me some silver?" "Yes, my dear,  I bring you some."

"Lov-er, you bring me some gold?" "Yes, my dear, I bring you some.   I

come   to town   to   see   you save,   save  you mus' be saved."

An' the lover bring a buggy an' carry her off an' save her life at
last.

An' the mumma say: "You never better, tuffa."[1]

*Jack Mantora me no choose any.*

From Andros Island, Bahamas, comes another Negro version,
likewise in *cante-fable* form, mingling prose narrative and singing.[2] It is very generally known throughout the islands. The
beginning and end will suffice to give its flavor.

Now, dis was a king had one daughter.  He sen' her to school in
anoder countree, an enchanted lan'.  He [she] been deah to school.
Fall in love wi' a schoolboy name of Jack.  Jack belongin' to dat
same place.  After get through her edication, she went back home.
Now, she become a beeg woman, time to beco' engaged.  De princess
son want to be engaged to her.  She won't accep' to her [him].  All
de high majorities she would n' accep' to none.  One day more 'n all,
she went out for a walk.  In walkin' she pick up a gold watch.  She
turn back home, she say, "O mommer! look what a beautiful present
I picked up!"  So her mother did n't stan'.  She make de alarm.
She say dat she steal it.  Dat de revenge 'cause would n' cote none
of dese high people.  In dose days dey don' put you to jail for stealin',
dey hang.  Dey make de gallows ready to be hung.  Dey took her
down where dey had de gallers rig.  An' deah she stud up.

---

[1] *You never better:* you will never be good for anything.  *Tuffa,* with Italian *u,* imi-
tates spitting, a sign of contempt.

[2] Elsie Clews Parsons, "Folk-Tales of Andros Island, Bahamas," *Memoirs American
Folk-Lore Society,* xiii, 152–154.

[Then follows the singing to the relatives one after the other, as in the other *cante-fables*, till the truelove comes.]

An' when he got to de place where was de gallers rig, he roll down one bag of gol'. He had two double team, — one wi' gol', one wi' silver. An' he took her down an' pay her one bag o' gol'. An' as she jump in de carriage, I was right alongside, an' I dart, knock me right here to tell you dat little lie.

In three English variants,[1] likewise, the ballad has become a tale that mingles prose and verse. The most dramatic of the three is from Yorkshire.[2] It is called "The Golden Ball."

A man gives a golden ball to each of two lasses, and if either loses the ball she is to be hanged. The younger, while playing with her ball, tosses it over a park paling; the ball runs away over the grass into a house, and is seen no more. Then the usual drama is acted out, the words of the girl being in verse, the rest of the narrative in prose.

Now t' lass was taken to York to be hanged. She was brought out on t' scaffold, and t' hangman said, "Now, lass, tha must hang by t' neck till tha be'st dead." But she cried out:

1. "Stop, stop! . . .

    I think I see my mother coming.

2. "Oh, mother, hast brought my golden ball,
    And come to set me free?"

3. "I 've neither brought thy golden ball,
    Nor come to set thee free,
    But I have come to see thee hung,
    Upon this gallows-tree."

[Then the hangman said], "Now, lass, say thy prayers, for tha must dee."

[1] Child, H*a*, H*b*, H*c*.

[2] Child, H*a*. Compare the closely resembling version, also from York, related under the title "The Golden Ball," in Joseph Jacobs, *More English Fairy Tales*, David Nutt, London, 1894, pp. 12-15.

4. "Stop, stop! . . .
. . . . . . .
I think I see my father coming.
. . . . . .

5. "O, father, hast brought my golden ball,
    And come to set me free?"
. . . . . . .
. . . . . . .

6. "I've neither brought thy golden ball,
    Nor come to set thee free,
But I have come to see thee hung,
    Upon this gallows-tree."

[The maid thinks she sees her brother coming, her sister, uncle, aunt, cousin. The hangman then says]:

"I ween't stop no longer, tha's making gam of me. Tha must be hung at once." But now she saw her sweetheart coming through the crowd, and he had over head i' t'air her own golden ball.

7. "Stop, stop! . . .
. . . . . . .
I see my sweetheart coming,
. . . . . .

8. "Sweetheart, hast brought my golden ball,
    And come to set me free?"
. . . . . . .
. . . . . . .

9. "Aye, I have brought thy golden ball,
    And come to set thee free;
I have not come to see thee hung,
    Upon this gallows-tree."

The last development of all, which ends many a ballad's strange eventful history, is when it loses its identity as a song and becomes a children's game. All that then remains is a dramatic skeleton of the original story, portrayed through simple action and appropriate gestures by children at play. Version *F* of "The Maid Freed from the Gallows," in Child, is a fragment that has reached this stage. A curious mixture of game and song was also observed in one of the slums of New York City in 1916.[1]

[1] G. L. Kittredge, "Ballads and Songs," *J. A. F. L.*, xxx, 319.

It was known to the children as the game of "The Golden Ball."
A prose dialogue, acted out, preceded the singing:

"Father, father, may I have my golden ball?"
"No, you may not have your golden ball."
"But all the other girls and boys have their golden balls."
"Then you may have your golden ball, but if you lose your golden
ball, you will hang on yonder rusty gallery."
"Father, father, I have lost my golden ball."
"Well, then, you will hang on yonder rusty gallery."

"Captain, captain, hold the rope;
  I hear my mother's voice.
Mother, have you come to set me free,
  Or have you come to see me hang
  On yonder rusty gallery?"
"No, I have come to see you hang
  On yonder rusty gallery."

[In the second stanza, the same dialogue is repeated, with the sister
taking the mothers place.]

"Captain, captain, hold the rope;
  I hear my baby's voice.
Baby, have you come to set me free,
  Or have you come to see me hang
On yonder rusty gallery?"
"Da, da."   (*Gives him the ball.*)

[Sometimes the last stanza ends, after the ballad fashion, with the
sweetheart:]

"Captain, captain, hold the rope;
  I hear my sweetheart's voice.
Sweetheart, have you come to set me free,
  Or have you come to see me hang
  On yonder rusty gallery?"

"Yes, I have brought your golden ball,
  And come to set you free;
I have not come to see you hanged
  On yonder rusty gallery."

In the game of "The Golden Ball," the wheel of the ballad
has come full circle. Composed before Chaucer's pilgrimage,
sung in England and Scotland during the spacious times of

Queen Elizabeth, recorded by the antiquarian scholar Bishop Thomas Percy in the days of George III, just before the American Revolution, scattered over most of the countries of Europe, crossing the Atlantic with the early settlers and still lingering in out-of-the-way places in both America and Great Britain, the ballad of "The Maid Freed from the Gallows" has in the end become a rustic English tale, a Negro *cante-fable* in the Bahamas and the West Indies, a playlet at a Negro school commencement, and a children's game in the slums of New York City. A long life and a varied one!

# SOUTH CAROLINA BALLADS

# I

## LADY ISABEL AND THE ELF KNIGHT

### (Child, No. 4)

Along with "Lord Randal," "Lord Thomas and Fair Elinor," "Lord Lovel," "Bonny Barbara Allen," and "The Hangman's Tree," this is one of the most widely distributed ballads in America. For American variants and references, see the head-note to this ballad in Cox, p. 3. Campbell and Sharp give five variants and five tunes; and Cox, nine variants and one tune.

The head-note in Kittredge speaks thus of its prevalence in Europe: "Of all the ballads, this has perhaps obtained the widest circulation. It is nearly as well known to the southern as to the northern nations of Europe. It has an extraordinary currency in Poland. The Germans, High and Low, and the Scandinavians, preserve it, in a full and evidently ancient form, even in the tradition of this generation." In some versions (as Child, A and B) the supernatural character of the Elf Knight is retained, in others it is lost completely, and he has become merely "False Sir John" or, as in our variant B, "Young Jimmie."

### A

Communicated by Mrs. John B. King of Williamston, S. C., in 1913. Mrs. King says: "I got these words from my mother. She learned it from her father when she was a small girl. It is the only song (I think she said) she ever heard her father sing."

1. She mounted on the bonny, bonny bright,
        And him on the dapple gray.
    They rid the length of a long summer's night,
        Three hours before day, day,
        Three hours before day.

2. "O light here, my pretty miss,
        O light here, my pretty miss, with me;
    For it's the six King's daughters I have drowned,
        And the seventh you shall be, be
        And the seventh that you shall be.

3. "O pull off your silk and satin,
        O pull off your silk," says he;
    "For it's too fine and costly for to rot
        In the salt-water sea, sea,
        For to rot in the salt-water sea."

4. "O whirl all around and around and about.
   With your face to the willow tree;
   For it is a shame and scandal to see
   A naked woman as me, me,
   A naked woman as me."

5. He whirled all around and around and about,
   And his face to the willow tree;
   She caught him by the small o' the back
   And tripped him in the salt-water sea, sea,
   And she tripped him in the salt-water sea.

6. "O catch me by your lily-white hands,
   And help me out of here;
   And all the promises I've made to you
   I'll double on the thirty-three, three,
   I'll double on the thirty-three."

7. "Lie there, lie there, you old villain,
   There where you wanted me.
   Lie there my false-hearted love,
   There where you wanted me, me,
   There where you wanted me."

8. She mounted on the bonny, bonny bright,
   And she led the dapple gray.
   She rid the length of a long summer's night
   Three hours before day, day,
   Three hours before day.

9. "O hold your tongue little parrot,
   Don't tell no tales on me;
   I'll kivver your cage in gold
   And your door in ivoree, ree,
   And your door in ivoree."

## B

"Young Jimmie." Communicated by Mrs. Fannie Brennecke, of Wal-
halla, S. C., Nov. 17, 1924. Mrs. Brennecke writes: "In a cabin on my father's
plantation, back in the Sixties, lived an old, old woman, known to all as
'Granny Rochester.' It was one of my greatest pleasures to visit at her cabin,
and have her sing to me this ludicrous song, entitled 'Young Jimmie,'
which to my childish fancy was most wonderful — the quintessence of
tragedy and pathos!

"If you have heard the old English ballad, 'Lord Lovel,' then you have
heard the tune by which Granny Rochester sang of the treacherous Jimmie,
crowding in or slurring the notes as it suited her fancy to fit the meter of
the verses. When she would sing the line: 'Ye'd take me away to the old
Scotland,' she would pronounce the word 'Scot-land,' emphasizing the two
syllables equally."

1. Young Jimmie, he was a brisk young lad,
    He came across the sea;
  He came across of a Saturday night,
    And then he came a-courting of me, me, me,
    And then he came a-courting of me.

2. He courted me a Saturday, he courted me a Sunday,
    He courted me the live long day;
  I had no heart for to flee from him,
    No tongue for to tell him nay, nay, nay,
    No tongue for to tell him nay.

3. He mounted on his milk-white steed,
    I rode my father's grey;
  And we rode away from the old Scotland
    Two hours before it came day, day, day,
    Two hours before it came day.

4. "Light off, light off, pretty Polly, my bride,
    Light off by the side of me;
  The six King's daughters I have drowned here,
    And the seventh thou shalt be, be, be,
    And the seventh thou shalt be!

5. "Take off that fine white silk satin robe
   And hang it on yon bush;
   For it is far too fine and cost-ilee
   For to rotten in the sea, sea, sea,
   For to rotten in the sea."

6. I turned my face toward the main,
   My back toward the lea —
   I threw my arms around his neck
   And cast him into the sea, sea, sea,
   And cast him into the sea!

7. "Take me out, take me out, pretty Polly, my bride,
   Take me out by the side of thee;
   The six King's daughters I have drowned here
   And the seventh's drowned me, me, me,
   And the seventh's drowned me!"

8. "Lie there, lie there, young Jimmie,
   'T was n't what ye promised me;
   Ye'd take me away to the old Scotland,
   And there ye'd marry me, me, me,
   And there ye'd marry me!"

9. I mounted on the milk-white steed,
   I led the dapple grey;
   And I rode away to my father's house
   Two hours before it came day, day, day,
   Two hours before it came day.

10. "Hush up, hush up, pretty Pollye, my bird,
    Don't ye tell no tales on me;
    I'll build ye a cage of the new Brittain gold,
    With the doors of ivoree, ree, ree,
    With the doors of ivoree!"

# II

## LORD RANDAL

### (CHILD, No. 12)

ONE of the most widely spread of American survivals. Many variants and tunes are reported from most of the states collecting ballads, and new copies keep coming in. Campbell and Sharp give five variants and five tunes; Cox reports twelve West Virginia variants; and Sharp, in England, records one variant ("Lord Rendel") and tune, saying of it: "This ballad is sung very freely from one end of the island to the other, and I have taken it down at least twenty times." See page xxv of his Introduction for other English references and characteristics. For further American references see *J. A. F. L.* and head-note in Cox, p. 23.

### *A*

"McDonald," from C. E. Means' article, "A Singular Literary Survival," *The Outlook*, September 9, 1899, pp. 119–122. This and a variant of "Lord Thomas and Fair Elinor" are quoted, and described as "two 'poor buckra' ballads."

1. "Whar have you been, McDonald, McDonald,
  Whar have you been, McDonald, my son?"
    "I have been out hunting mother —
    Make my bed soon!
    I'm a weary, weary wanderer,
    In a pain to lie down."

2. "Whar are your greyhounds, McDonald, McDonald,
  Whar are your greyhounds, McDonald, my son?"
    "They are still out sunning, mother —
    Make my bed soon!
    I'm a weary, weary wanderer,
    In a pain to lie down."

3. "Whar did you get your dinner, McDonald, McDonald,
  Whar did you get your dinner, McDonald, my son?"
    "I dined with my sweetheart —
    Mother, make my bed soon;
    I'm a weary, weary wanderer,
    In a pain to lie down."

4. "What did you have for dinner, McDonald, McDonald,
   What did you have for dinner, McDonald, my son?"
     "We had white fish and poison —
     Mother, make my bed soon;
     I'm a weary, weary wanderer,
     In a pain to lie down."

5. "What will you will your father, McDonald, McDonald,
   What will you will your father, McDonald, my son?"
     "I will him my gold staff —
     Mother, make my bed soon;
     I'm a weary, weary wanderer,
     In a pain to lie down."

6. "What will you will your mother, McDonald, McDonald,
   What will you will your mother, McDonald, my son?"
     "I will her my gold watch —
     Mother, make my bed soon;
     I'm a weary, weary wanderer,
     In a pain to lie down."

7. "What will you will your sister, McDonald, McDonald,
   What will you will your sister, McDonald, my son?"
     "I will her my jewelry —
     Mother, make my bed soon;
     I'm a weary, weary wanderer,
     In a pain to lie down."

8. "What will you will your sweetheart, McDonald, McDonald,
   What will you will your sweetheart, McDonald, my son?"
     "I will her a keg of powder
     To blow her sky-high!
     For I'm a weary, weary wanderer,
     In a pain to lie down."

## *B*

"Poor Anzo." Communicated by Mrs. John B. King, of Williamston, S.C., in 1913. This variant is interesting because of its manifold and peculiar perversions. Practically everything that could befall a ballad in oral tradition has happened to it. In this respect it deserves to rank as a classic!

1. "Where have you been, poor Anzo, my son?
      Where have you been, poor Anzo, my son?"
   "I have been out a-hunting; make by bed soon;
      I am sick in my heart, I should fail and lie down."

2. "What did you leave your dear father for, Anzo, my son?
      What did you leave your dear father for, Anzo, my son?"
   "He has six head of horses; make my bed soon;
      I am sick in my heart, I should fail and lie down."

3. "What did you leave your dear mother for, Anzo, my son?
      What did you leave your dear mother for, Anzo, my son?"
   "She has plenty of kitchen furniture; make my bed soon;
      I am sick in my heart, I should fail and lie down."

4. "What did you leave your dear sister for, Anzo, my son?
      What did you leave your dear sister for, Anzo, my son?"
   "She has . . . ; make my bed soon;
      For I am sick in my heart, I should fail and lie down."

5. "What did you leave your dear sweetheart for, Anzo, my
         son?
      What did you leave your dear sweetheart for, Anzo, my
         son?"
   "Here is a red-hot iron will broil a bone brown,
      She is the cause of my lying down."

6. "What will you have for supper, poor Anzo, my son?
      What will you have for supper, poor Anzo, my son?"
   "Make me a little breely broth soup,
      For I am sick in my heart, I should fail and lie down."

# III

## YOUNG BEICHAN

### (CHILD, No. 53)

CAMPBELL and Sharp give five variants and five tunes; Cox gives four variants and refers to a fifth; Sharp prints a good text and tune, remarking (Notes, p. xix): "This, again, is a very popular ballad with English folk-singers, and I have noted down nineteen different versions of it." His discussion of the origin and history of the plot may be interestingly compared with the account given in Kittredge's head-note, p. 95. For English references, see Sharp, p. xix, and for American references, Cox's head-note, p. 36.

"Lord Bateman," communicated by Miss Ada Taylor Graham, of Columbia, S. C., Dec. 28, 1924. "I have never seen it in any collection," writes Miss Graham, "nor have I ever heard it sung except by my mother and grandmother, who had learned it from my grandfather's mother."

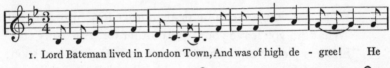

1. Lord Bateman lived in London Town, And was of high de - gree! He

swore he could not rest a min - ute Till he had sail - ed o'er the sea.

1. Lord Bateman lived in London Town,
   And was of high degree!
   He swore he could not rest a minute
   Till he had sailed o'er the sea.

2. He sailed east, he sailed west;
   He sailed to a far countree,
   Where he was taken and put in prison
   Where he could neither hear nor see.

3. His keeper had an only daughter,
   And she was of a high degree.
   She stole the key's of her father's prison
   And swore she'd set Lord Bateman free.

4. ·   ·   ·   ·   ·   ·   ·

5. And there they made a solemn vow,
    For seven long years they let it stand;
  That he should marry no other woman,
    And she should marry no other man.

6. .    .    .    .    .    .    .    .

7. When seven long years had rolled away,
    And another year had fully come,
  She packed up all her gay rich clothing
    And went to seek for Lord Bateman.

8. .    .    .    .    .    .    .    .

9. She knocked so loud, she knocked so clearly
    She made the castle gates to ring.
  "Oh, who is there?" cried the brisk young porter,
    "Who's there a-waiting to come in?"

10. She asked, "Is this Lord Bateman's castle?
    And is Lord Bateman now within?"
  "Ah yes! ah yes!" cried the brisk young porter,
    "He and his bride have just come in."

11. "Go ask him for a piece of bread,
    And ask him for some wine so strong,
  And ask him if he still remembers
    Who freed him from his iron bonds."

12. .    .    .    .    .    .    .    .
    "At your gate stands the fairest lady
  That my two eyes have ever seen.

13. "She has a ring on every finger,
    And on the middle one she has three,
  And round her neck is a golden necklace
    Fit for the bride and company.

14. "She asks you for a piece of bread,
    She asks you for some wine so strong,
  She asks you if you still remember
    Who freed you from your iron bonds."

15. .    .    .    .    .    .    .    .

16. He smote his fist upon the table,
    And broke it into pieces three,
    Crying, "Ah I know, I know that lady,
    Her name it must be Susy Free."

17. .    .    .    .    .    .    .    .

18. .    .    .    .    .    .    .    .
    "I brought her here on a horse and saddle,
    I'll send her away in a coach and three."

19. Then he took Susie Free by the lily-white hand,
    And he led her o'er the threshold stone,
    Saying, "Now your name it shall be changed
    Your name shall now be Lady Bateman."

# IV

## YOUNG HUNTING

### (CHILD, No. 68)

CAMPBELL and Sharp give six variants and six tunes; Cox gives two variants. For other American variants and references, see Cox's head-note, p. 42. This ballad is known in America, usually, as "Lord Henry," "Love Henry," or "Loving Henry." The girl's name is generally Lady Margaret.

"The Old Scotch Well," or "Little Scotchee." Communicated by Miss Tressie Pierce, of Columbia, S. C., who learned it in Alexander County, North Carolina.

1. "Light, light, light, my lit-tle Scotch-ee, And stay all night with me; I have a bed of the ver-y, ver-y best, I'll give it up to thee, I'll give it up to thee."

(a) VERSES 2, 3, 4, 5, 6 AND 8

2. "I can-not light, and I will not light, And

1. "Light, light, light, my little Scotch-ee,
    And stay all night with me;
  I have a bed of the very, very best,
      I'll give it up to thee,
      I'll give it up to thee."

2. "I cannot light, and I will not light,
      And stay all night with thee;
   For there's a girl in the old Scotch Yard,
      This night a-waiting for me,
      This night a-waiting for me."

3. "You cannot light, and you will not light,
      But from me you'll never part;"
   She took a pen-knife from her side,
      And pierced him in the heart,
      And pierced him in the heart.

4. She called unto her little lady miss,
      "Come unto me I say;
   For there's a dead man in my bed,
      Come carry him away,
      Come carry him away."

5. She called unto her little lady miss,
      "Count the hours, one, two, three;
   Are the chickens a-crowing for the middle of the night,
      Or are they a-crowing for day,
      Or are they a-crowing for day?"

6. Some took him by the lily-white hand,
      Some took him by the feet,
   And threw him into a new-dug well,
      Some forty feet deep,
      Some forty feet deep.

7. "Light, light, light, my little birdie,
      And settle on my knee;
   I have a cage of the very, very best,
      I'll give it up to thee,
      I'll give it up to thee."

8. "I cannot light, and I will not light,
      And settle on your knee;
   For I'm afraid you will sarve me like you sarved,
      Your little Scotch-ee,
      Your little Scotch-ee."

# V

# LORD THOMAS AND FAIR ANNET

## (CHILD, No. 73)

CHILD gives ten versions. His Version A is Scottish, and is entitled Lord Thomas and Fair Annet. It consists of thirty stanzas and is taken from Percy's *Reliques*. Child justly describes it as "one of the most beautiful of all ballads." Child's Version D, containing 19 stanzas, is of English origin, and is the version which has since become traditional both in Great Britain and America. It likewise is taken from Percy's *Reliques*, where it bears the title "A Tragical Ballad on the Unfortunate Love of Lord Thomas and Fair Ellinor, together with the Downfall of the Browne Girl." Percy took it from the Pepys collection made in the time of Charles II, when it was licensed as a broadside by L'Estrange, who was censor from 1663 to 1685. Child's version I, entitled "Fair Annie and Sweet Willie" and consisting of 41 stanzas, comes from the Scotch ballad material which Scott collected for *Minstrelsy of the Scottish Border*.

"Lord Thomas and Fair Elinor" is still widely prevalent both in Great Britain and America. It occurs in many variants in all of the Southern states as well as in New England and various parts of the West. In fact, with the sole exception of Barbara Allen, it is the most widely distributed of all the ballads surviving in America.

Campbell and Sharp give eleven texts and eleven tunes, and Cox gives nine texts and mentions two others. Sharp gives one full text and tune, and refers to this as a very common ballad. He notes that the three lines between the twentieth and twenty-first stanzas of his variant are always spoken and never sung. The lines are:

> Make me a grave both long and wide,
> And lay fair Ellinor by my side —
> And the brown girl at my feet.

"This is the only instance of the kind," he adds, "that I have come across."

For additional English versions and references, see Sharp's note, p. xxviii; and for American versions and references, see Cox's head-note, pp. 45, 46.

The rôle of villainess assigned to the brown girl in all versions of the ballad is but another instance of the marked preference shown for blondes rather than for brunettes in all forms of Germanic folk-lore, tale and song alike. About the only exception to blonde unanimity in either artistic or popular early English poetry is the anonymous poem "The Nutbrowne Maide," dating from about 1500, in which the maid who is selected to prove the case of a woman's constancy is, as the title indicates, a thorough brunette.

Like so many other ballads which recount love's tragedy, Lord Thomas and Fair Elinor closes with the intertwining rose and brier from the lovers' graves, a motif which serves as the tragic counterpart of "And they lived happily ever after."

*A*

"Lord Thomas and Fair Elinor." Communicated by Mr. W. B. Compton, from Aiken County, S. C., Nov. 5, 1913. He stated that it was transcribed by Mrs. Alice Day Compton "to whom it was sung by her mother Mrs. Martha O'Neall Day, who was born in 1829, and who learned it when a girl."

1. Lord Thomas rode up to Fair Elinor's gate, And there he did knock and ring. There was no one so ready as Fair Elinor To let Lord Thomas come in.

2. "What news! What news! Lord Thomas?" she cried. "What news have you brought unto me?" "I have come to invite you to my wedding. That will be sad news unto thee."

1. Lord Thomas rode up to Fair Elinor's gate,
   And there he did knock and ring.
   There was no one so ready as Fair Elinor
   To let Lord Thomas come in.

2. "What news!  What news!  Lord Thomas?" she cried.
   "What news have you brought unto me?"
   "I have come to invite you to my wedding.
   That will be sad news unto thee."

3. She dressed herself in rich array;
   Her garments were all of green;
   And every town that she passed through,
   They took her to be some queen.

4. Fair Elinor rode up to Lord Thomas's gate,
    And then she did knock and ring.
  There was no one so ready as Lord Thomas,
    To let Fair Elinor in.

5. "Is this your bride, Lord Thomas?" she cried;
    "Methinks she is wondrous brown.
  When you might have had as fair a lady,
    As ever the sun shone on."

6. This brown girl having a knife in her hand,
    Which was both keen and sharp.
  Between the short rib and the long,
    She wounded Fair Elinor's heart.

7. "Oh! are you blind, Lord Thomas," she cried.
    "Or care you nothing for me,
  That you stand and see my precious heart's blood,
    Come trickling down to my knee?"

8. Lord Thomas having a sword at his side,
    Which was made of a metal so free.
  He cut his wife's head off of her body,
    And threw it against a tree.

9. And then he planted the hilt in the dust,
    The point towards his heart.
  And there never were three true lovers met,
    As quick as these three did part.

### B

"Lord Thomas and Fair Eleanor." Communicated by Miss Katharine Drayton Mayrant Simons, of Summerville, S. C., who gives the following account of it:

"This ballad has always been one of the nursery songs in our family and my earliest recollection of it is as sung by my grandmother, Harriet Hyrne Simons of Charleston. The verses of it which I inclose are sung still to-day by my grandfather, father and aunts. With the exception of Professor Compton's version, printed in your article, I have never seen the ballad in writing, but have it only by memory as it has come down through generations in the family. My grandfather, William Simons of Charleston, re-

members it as sung by his mother. The version I send you I wrote off from
memory, and submitted for correction and corroboration to the members of
my family who still remember and sing it. The ballad as I have written it
off has been sung for at least a century in the Simons family of Charleston."
This variant very closely resembles Child's Version D.

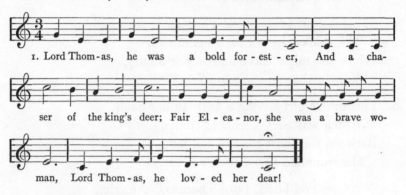

1. Lord Thomas, he was a bold forester, And a chaser of the king's deer; Fair Eleanor, she was a brave woman, Lord Thomas, he loved her dear!

1. Lord Thomas, he was a bold forester,
    And a chaser of the king's deer;
    Fair Eleanor, she was a brave woman,
    Lord Thomas, he loved her dear!

2. "Now, riddle my riddle, dear Mother," he cried,
    "And riddle it all into one;
    For whether to marry the Fair Eleanor,
    Or bring you the Brown Girl home?"

3. "The Brown Girl, she hath both houses and lands,
    Fair Eleanor, she hath none;
    Therefore I charge you, upon my blessing,
    To bring me the Brown Girl home!"

4. He clothed himself in gallant attire,
    His merrymen all in green;
    And every borough that he rode thorough,
    They took him to be some king.

5. And, when he reached Fair Eleanor's bower,
    He knocked thereat, therein,
    And, who so ready as Fair Eleanor
    To let Lord Thomas in?

6. "What news?  What news, Lord Thomas?" she cried,
   "What news dost thou bring unto me?"
   "I come to bid thee to my wedding,
   And that is sad news for thee!"

7. "Now Heaven forbid, Lord Thomas," she cried,
   "That any such thing should be done!
   I thought to have been, myself, the bride,
   And thou to have been the bridegroom!"

8. "Now, riddle my riddle, dear Mother," she cried,
   "And riddle it all into one.
   For whether I go to Lord Thomas's wedding,
   Or whether I tarry at home?"

9. "There be many that be thy friend, Daughter,
   But a thousand be thy foe:
   Therefore I charge thee, upon my blessing,
   To Lord Thomas's wedding don't go!"

10. "There be many that be my friend, Mother,
    Though a thousand be my foe:
    So, betide my life, betide my death,
    To Lord Thomas's wedding I'll go!"

11. She decked herself in gallant attire,
    Her tiremen all in green;
    And every borough that she rode thorough,
    They took her to be some queen.

12. And, when she reached Lord Thomas's door,
    She knocked thereat, therein;
    And who so ready as Lord Thomas
    To let Fair Eleanor in?

13. "Be this your bride, Lord Thomas?" she cried.
    "Methinks she looks wondrous brown!
    Thou mightest have had as fair a woman
    As ever the sun shone on!"

14. "Despise her not, Fair Ellen!" he cried.
        "Despise her not unto me!
    For better I love thy little finger
        Than all of her whole body!"

15. The Brown Girl, she had a little pen-knife,
        Which was both long and sharp;
    And between the broad ribs and the short,
        She pierced Fair Eleanor's heart!

16. "O art thou blind, Lord Thomas?" she cried.
        "Or canst thou not plainly see
    My own heart's blood run trickling down,
        Run trickling down to my knee?"

17. Lord Thomas, he had a sword at his side,
        And, as he walked up the hall,
    He cut the bride's head from her shoulders
        And flung it against the wall!

18. He placed the hilt against the ground,
        The point against his heart!
    So, never three lovers together did meet,
        And sooner again did part!

19. They buried Fair Ellen beneath an oak tree,
        Lord Thomas beneath the church spire;
    And out of her bosom there grew a red rose,
        And out of her lover's a briar!

20. They grew and they grew, till they reached the church top;
        They grew till they reached the church spire;
    And there they entwined in a true-lover's-knot,
        For true-lovers all to admire!

## C

"The Brown Girl or Fair Eleanor." Communicated by Miss Tressie Pierce, of Columbia, S. C., who learned it in Alexander County, N. C.

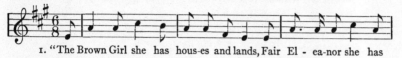

1. "The Brown Girl she has hous-es and lands, Fair El - ea-nor she has

none; The best ad - vice I can give you, my son, Is to

bring the Brown Girl home, Is to bring the Brown Girl home."

1. "The Brown Girl she has houses and lands,
   Fair Eleanor she has none;
   The best advice I can give you, my son,
   Is to bring the Brown Girl home,
   Is to bring the Brown Girl home."

2. He dressed himself in scarlet red,
   And rode all over the town;
   And everybody that saw him that day,
   Thought he was the King.

3. He rode till he came to Fair Eleanor's door,
   And tingled at the ring;
   And none so ready as Fair Eleanor,
   To arise and let him in.

4. "What news, what news, Lord Thomas," she said,
   "What news have you for me?"
   "I've come to ask you to my weddin'.
   To-morrow is the day.
   To-morrow is the day."

5. "Bad news, bad news, Lord Thomas," she said,
     "Bad news, to me;
   You've come to ask me to your weddin',
     When I thought your bride I was to be."

6. She dressed herself in scarlet red,
     And rode all over the town;
   And everybody that saw her that day,
     Took her to be the Queen,
     Took her to be the Queen.

7. She rode till she came to Lord Thomas's door,
     And tingled at the ring;
   And none as ready as Lord Thomas himself,
     To arise and let her in.

8. "Is this your bride, Lord Thomas," she cried,
     "I'm sure, she's wonderful Brown;
   You might have had as fair a young bride,
     As ever the sun shone on,
     As ever the sun shone on."

9. The Brown Girl, she had a long pen-knife,
     'T was wonderful long and sharp;
   Between the short ribs and the long,
     She pierced Fair Eleanor's heart,
     She pierced Fair Eleanor's heart.

10. "Fair Eleanor, what makes you look so pale?
      You used to look so red;
    You used to have two rosy red cheeks,
      And now you've nary one,
      And now you've nary one."

11. "Oh, don't you see, or can't you see,
      The knife that was pierced in me?
    Oh don't you see my own heart's blood,
      A-tricklin' to my knee,
      A-tricklin' to my knee?"

12. Lord Thomas had a long broad-sword,
       It was wonderful long and sharp,
     He cut the head of the Brown Girl off,
       And kicked it against the wall,
       And kicked it against the wall.

13. "Go dig my grave under yonders green tree,
       Go dig it wide and long;
     And bury Fair Eleanor in my arms,
       And the Brown Girl at my feet,
       And the Brown Girl at my feet."


### D

"Lord Thomas and Fa'r Elinor." From C. E. Means's article, "A Singular Literary Survival," *The Outlook*, Sept. 9, 1899, pp. 119–122. This and a variant of "Lord Randal" (quoted above, variant A, p. 101) are described as "two 'poor buckra' ballads."

1. Lord Thomas rode up to fa'r Elinor's door,
       And tingled on the ring.
     There was none so ready as fa'r Elinor herself
       To let Lord Thomas in.

2. "What news, what news?" fair Elinor cried,
       "What news, what news?" cried she.
     "I've come to ask you to my wedding."
       "Oh, very bad news!" said she.

3. "Come mother, oh mother, riddle these words,
       O riddle this riddle for me;
     Shall I go to Lord Thomas's wedding,
       Or tarry at home with thee?"

4. "I'll riddle your riddle," her mother said,
       "I'll riddle the riddle in three:
     Don't go to Lord Thomas's wedding,
       But tarry at home with me."

5. Fair Elinor dressed herself in white,
     Her servants she dressed in green;
   And as they rode through all the towns
     They took her to be some queen.

6. She rode up to Lord Thomas's door,
     And tingled on the ring;
   There was none so ready as Lord Thomas himself
     To let fair Elinor in.

7. He took her by her lily-white hand
     And led her up the hall,
   And thar he sot her at the head of the bed,
     Amongst the neighbors all.

8. "Is this your bride?" fair Elinor cried.
     "Why, she looks wonderful brown.
   You might have married as fair a girl
     As ever the sun shone on."

9. The brown gal had a little pen-knife,
     It was both keen and small,
   She stuck it in fair Elinor's heart,
     Amongst the neighbors all.

10. Lord Thomas had a little keen sword,
     It was both keen and small;
   He took and cut off the brown gal's head
     And kicked it against the wall.

11. And he went shuffeling over the floor,
     The pint stuck in his breast.
   Was ever three earthly lovers so soon
     Sent to their heavenly rest?

## ε

"The Brown Girl or Fair Ellender." Communicated by Mrs. Emma Clement, Spartanburg County, Dec. 8, 1913.

1. "Mother, dear mother, come riddle to me,
       Come riddle all as one;
   It's must I marry fair Ellender,
       Or bring the Brown girl home?"

2. "The Brown girl she has a house and home,
       Fair Ellender has none;
   Therefore I'd seek you with my own blessing
       The Brown girl you bring home."

3. "Mother, dear mother, come riddle to me,
       Come riddle all as one;
   It's must I go to Low Thomas's wedding,
       Or tarry with you at home?"

4. "You know you have a-many a friend,
       You know you have a foe;
   Therefore I'd seek you with my own blessing
       To Low Thomas's wedding don't go."

5. She dressed herself in pearl of gold,
       She dressed herself in green;
   And every town that she rode through
       She was taken to be some queen.

6. "Low Thomas, Low Thomas, is this your bride?
       I pray she looks very brown;
   You could have gotten as fair a lady
       As ever the sun shone on."

7. The Brown girl she had a little penny-knife,
       It was both keen and sharp;
   Between the long ribs and the short ones
       She pressed fair Ellender's heart.

8. "Fair Ellender, fair Ellender,
      What makes you look so pale?
   I thought you bore as high a color
      As any other female?"

9. "Low Thomas, Low Thomas, are you blind,
      Or can't you very well see?
   For don't you see my own heart blood
      Come streaming down my knees?"

10. He took the Brown girl by the hand,
      And led her through the hall;
   He drew his sword, cut off her head,
      And kicked it against the wall.

11. He pointed the handle toward the sun,
      The point toward his breast.
   Here is the going of three true loves,
      God send our souls to rest.

### F

"Lord Thomas." A variant of sixteen stanzas communicated by Mrs. Ida
Cooley King, of Williamston, S. C., in 1913.

# VI

## LORD LOVEL

### (Child, No. 75)

This ballad is very common all through the South, sharing honors in this respect with "Barbara Allen," "The Hangman's Tree," "Lady Isabel and the Elf Knight," and "Lord Thomas and Fair Elinor." It is also found widely in New England, where Mr. Phillips Barry reports finding six melodies. It is likewise reported from many places in the West.

Its popularity in America, however, like that of "Barbara Allen," can not be traced entirely to oral tradition. "Lord Lovel" was printed in American song-books five times between 1836 and 1865, besides being issued several times in broadside form. For specific references, see Cox's head-note, p. 78, where are also listed other American texts, including comic and satirical variants, and parodies; and see also A. H. Tolman, *J. A. F. L.*, vol. xxix, p. 160, and note. There are five American manuscript texts among the Child manuscripts in Harvard University, in addition to the ten versions which are printed in Child's collection.

The tune published in Sharp is the same as that reproduced below. In regard to it, Sharp remarks: "I do not know of any publication in which the tune of this ballad is published." He speaks of having collected six versions in England but only one complete set of words. It would seem fairly certain that "Lord Lovel" is to-day much commoner in the United States than in Great Britain, as is also true of "Barbara Allen" and "The Hangman's Tree." It has a wide currency in South Carolina and elsewhere as a nursery song.

"Lord Lovel," by the way, clearly shows how necessary it is to deal with ballads as songs and not merely as poems. The text of "Lord Lovel" is sad and mournful. The tune, however, is lilting and rollicking, and with the triple repetition of the last word of the fourth line, turns the tear into a smile. The difference between reading it as a poem and singing it as a song is the difference between tragedy and comedy.

"Lord Lovel" is one of an interesting group of ballads which are usually classed together on account of similarities of plot, structure, and tone. The others are "Lord Thomas and Fair Elinor," "Fair Margaret and Sweet William," "Lady Alice or Giles Collins," and "Bonny Barbara Allen." All unfold a love story of man and maid, and all end tragically.

### *A*

"Lord Lovel." The melody was communicated by W. R. Dehon, of Summerville, S. C., in 1913. The text was contributed by Miss Caroline S. Dickinson. Mr. Dehon's text (listed as variant B) is almost exactly the same, except that it lacks one important stanza, the seventh, for which reason Miss Dickinson's text is printed next to the melody, which seems to be the standard tune everywhere for this ballad.

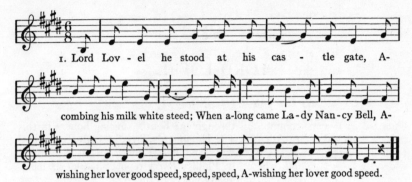

1. Lord Lov-el he stood at his cas-tle gate, A-combing his milk white steed; When a-long came La-dy Nan-cy Bell, A-wishing her lover good speed, speed, speed, A-wishing her lover good speed.

1. Lord Lovel he stood at his castle gate,
    A-combing his milk white steed;
   When along came Lady Nancy Bell,
    A-wishing her lover good speed, speed, speed,
    A-wishing her lover good speed.

2. "Oh where are you going, Lord Lovel?" she said;
    "Oh where are you going?" said she.
   "I'm going, my dear Lady Nancy Bell,
    Strange countries for to see, see, see,
    Strange countries for to see."

3. "When will you be back, Lord Lovel?" she said;
    "When will you be back?" said she.
   "In a year or two or three at the most
   I'll return to my Lady Nancee, cee, cee,
    I'll return to my Lady Nancee."

4. He'd not been gone but a year and a day,
    Strange countries for to see,
   When languishing thoughts came into his mind
    Lady Nancy Bell he would see.

5. He rode and he rode on his milk white steed,
    Till he reached fair London Town;
   And there he heard St. Varney's bell
    And the people all mourning around.

6. "Is any one dead?" Lord Lovel he said;
   "Is any one dead?" said he.
"A lady is dead," the people all said,
   "And they call her the Lady Nancy."

7. He ordered the grave to be opened forthwith,
   The shroud to be folded down;
And then he kissed her clay-cold lips
   Till the tears came trickling down.

8. Lady Nancy she died as it might be today,
   Lord Lovel he died tomorrow.
Lady Nancy she died of pure, pure grief,
   Lord Lovel he died of sorrow.

9. Lady Nancy was laid in St. Clement's churchyard,
   Lord Lovel was buried close by her;
And out of her bosom there grew a red rose,
   And out of his backbone a briar.

## *B*

"Lord Lovel." Described by Leonard L. Mackall in a letter to Professor Kittredge, dated Georgetown, S. C., Dec. 11, 1904. The first stanza runs:

Lord Lovel, he stood at his castle gate,
   A-combing his milk-white steed;
Lady Nancy Belle came riding by,
   A-wishing her lover good speed.

## *C*

"Lord Lovel." Communicated by W. R. Dehon, of Summerville, S. C., in 1913. Same as variant A except that stanza seven of A is lacking.

## D

"Lord Lovel." Submitted by Miss Ada Taylor Graham, of Columbia, S. C., December 28, 1924.

(Stanzas 1 to 5 same as in A)

6. "Oh, who is dead?" Lord Lovel, he said,
    "Oh, who is dead?" said he.
   "A lady is dead," the people all said,
    "And they call her the Lady Nancy."

7. He straightway ordered a grave to be made,
    And the coffin opened wide;
   And there by the side of Nancy Bell
    He laid him down and died.

8. They buried them both by the old church tower;
    They buried them side by side;
   And out of her grave there grew a red rose,
    And out of his a briar.

9. They grew and they grew on the old church tower,
    Till they could n't grow up any higher;
   And there they tied in a true lover's knot,
    For all true lovers to admire.

## E

"Lord Lovel." Communicated by Miss Belle Turner, of Richland County, S. C., in 1913. A variant of ten stanzas.

# VII

## LITTLE MUSGRAVE AND LADY BARNARD

### (CHILD, No. 81)

Kittredge's head-note mentions the fact that this ballad is quoted in Beaumont and Fletcher's "Knight of the Burning Pestle" (about 1611), Act V, Scene 3, and in other old plays; and that "Little Musgrave" is entered to Francis Coules in the Stationers' Registers, June 24, 1630.

See also, Professor Kittredge's four texts, *J. A. F. L.*, vol. xxx, pp. 309-317.

Campbell and Sharp give eight variants and eight tunes. Cox records only one stanza from West Virginia, but gives a variant secured from Kentucky. Both of the variants given below are fragmentary.

### A

"Little Matty Grove." Communicated by Mrs. John B. King, of Williamston, S. C., in 1913, who wrote that the singer she secured it from had great difficulty in recalling the exact words, and frequently had to resort to prose comments to fill out the story. The text is consequently fragmentary.

1. Lord Donald's wife went out to town
    To hear the Holy Word;
   Little footpage was standing near,
    A-listening what was said.

2. He heard her ask Little Matty Grove
    To go home with her tonight,
   To bed with her tonight.

   .    .    .    .    .    .    .

3. He run, he run to the broad riverside,
    And tuck to his belly and swum.

   .    .    .    .    .    .    .

   .    .    .    .    .    .    .

4. "Lord Donald, your wife went out to town to-day,
    To hear the Holy Word;
   And I heard her ask Little Matty Grove
    To go home with her tonight,
    To bed with her tonight."

5. "If this is a lie you've told to me
    I'll hang you to a tree;
  And if this is the truth you've told to me,
    My daughter your bride shall be."

6. .    .    .    .    .    .    .
    "I hear Lord Donald's horn a-blowing,
  A-coming over the hill."
     .    .    .    .    .    .    .

7. "Lie still, lie still, Little Matty Grove,
    And go to sleep;
  It's nothing but papa's little shipping boys
    A-driving the lambs to the ford."

8. From that they fell to a chat of talk,
    From that to a doze of sleep,
  . . . When they woke,
    Lord Donald was standing at the feet.

9. "It's how do you like my bed?" he says;
    "And how do you like my sheet?
  And how do you like my gay lady
    A-lying in your arms asleep?"

10. "I like your bed very well, Lord Donald,
    And I like your sheet;
  But I think more of your gay lady,
    A-lying in my arms asleep."

11. "Rise you up, Little Matty Grove,
    And draw on your fine suit;
  For I don't want it said, when I am dead,
    That I slewed a naked man."

12. (Here the singer recalls that Lord Donald had two very fine swords and gave Little Matty Grove the best sword, as well as the first stroke.)

13. And very the first lick was Little Matty Grove's;
    He caused the blood to run;
  The very next lick was Lord Donald's,
    He drove Little Matty Grove to the floor.

14. He set his gay lady on his knee,
(Asking her whom she loved best, Little Matty Grove or him.)

15. "I think very well of you, Lord Donald,
     I think very well of your kin;
     But I think heap more of Little Matty Grove
     Than I do of you and your kin."

16. (He kills her, but singer could recall none of the exact words.)

17. (In the next and final stanza, the tune unexpectedly changes to a very
    gay measure.)

18. "O don't you hear them little birds sing?
     O don't you hear them cry?
     Lord Donald has killed two people today,
     And tomorrow he must die, die,
     And tomorrow he must die."


## B

"Little Matthew Groves."    Communicated in 1925 by Miss Tressie
Pierce, of Columbia, S. C., who learned it in Alexander County, N. C.

1. High, and a high, and a high holiday,
    Upon the very first of the year;
    Little Matthew Groves started out to the church,
    The holy word for to hear,
    The holy word for to hear.

2. First passed him by a gay young bride,
    And the next passed him by was a pearl;
    And the third passed him by was Lord Donald's wife,
    The fairest of the three.

3. "Come along with me, little Matthew," she said;
    "This night in my arms for to lie;"
    "Oh no, oh no," he said, "I dare not for my life,
    For I know by the gold rings on your fingers
    That you are Lord Donald's wife."

4. "And what if I am Lord Donald's wife,
   Lord Donald is not at home;
   He's gone to the new academy,
   King Henry for to see."

5. A little foot page was standing by,
   And he took to his heels and he run;
   He came to where the bridge was broke,
   And he pitched on his breast and he swum.

6. He ran till he came to King Henry's gate,
   And tingled at the ring;
   And none so ready as Lord Donald himself,
   To get up and let him in.

7. "What news, what news, my little foot page,
   What news have you for me?"
   "Little Matthew Groves is at your own house
   In bed with your gay lady."

# VIII

## BONNY BARBARA ALLEN

### (CHILD, No. 84)

OF all the ballads in America "Barbara Allen" leads both in number of versions, number of tunes, and in geographical distribution. It is found all over the United States. As in the case of "Lord Lovel," its wide American popularity is not due entirely to oral tradition, but in certain measure to print. This ballad has appeared in ten song books and several broadsides. See A. H. Tolman, "Some Songs Traditional in the United States," *J. A. F. L.*, vol. xxix, p. 60, note 2; and G. L. Kittredge, "Ballads and Songs," *J. A. F. L.*, vol. xxx, p. 317. It was first published in America in the *American Songster*, Baltimore, 1836, and next in the *Southern Warbler*, Charleston, 1845.

Recently, it was included in *Heart Songs*, Boston, 1909. This collection of old favorites was the result of a contest in musical popularity conducted by the *National Magazine*, and is described as "contributed by 25,000 people."

The tunes "Barbara Allen" is sung to are as varied as its texts. Six different airs are recorded from New England, and many from all the Southern States, all differing not only from each other, but from the Scotch melody in Thomson's *Select Melodies of Scotland*, 1822, and the English air in Duncan's *The |Minstrelsy of England*, 1905. The two South Carolina melodies printed below are entirely different, as are the tunes in *Heart Songs* and in Campbell and Sharp.

"Bonny Barbara Allen" was first printed in England in *The Tea-Table Miscellany*, 1740, and next in Percy's *Reliques*, 1765. The same year, 1765, Goldsmith wrote in his third essay: "The music of the finest singer is dissonance to what I felt when our old dairy-maid sung me into tears with 'Johnnie Armstrong's Last Goodnight,' or 'The Cruelty of Barbara Allen.'" It was, however, known at least a hundred years earlier. Pepys makes the following reference to it in his Diary under the date of January 2, 1666: "In perfect pleasure I was to hear her [Mrs. Knipp, an actress] sing, and especially her little Scotch song of 'Barbara Allen.'" There is no way of telling how much earlier the song was composed, for of course neither the first appearance of a ballad in print nor the first published contemporary reference to it has any necessary relation to its age. A ballad may be current in oral tradition several hundred years before it gets into print. Or, for that matter, it may arise, flourish, and die out without being recorded in writing at all, and thus disappear without leaving a trace of its ever having existed.

Campbell and Sharp give ten texts and ten tunes, and Cox gives nine full texts and describes three others. Sharp gives a good text and tune, and speaks of the ballad's English prevalence as follows: "There is no ballad that country singers are more fond of than of 'Barbara Ellen,' or 'Barbarous Ellen,' or 'Edelin,' as it is usually called. I have taken down as many as twenty-seven variants." For other English references, see Sharp, Notes, p. xx; and for American references, see Cox's head-note, p. 96.

*A*

"Barbara Allen." Communicated by Mr. W. B. Compton, of Aiken County, S. C., in 1913. Mr. Compton says of it: "These old songs have been rehearsed from time to time by Mrs. Alice Day Compton, to whom they were sung by her mother, Mrs. Martha O'Neall Day, who was born in 1829." This variant consists of twelve stanzas, which are printed as six to conform to the melody. It most nearly resembles Child's Version B, which was taken from Percy's *Reliques*.

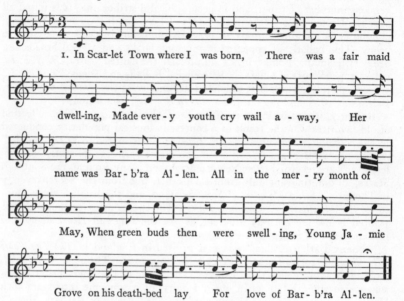

1. In Scar-let Town where I was born, There was a fair maid dwell-ing, Made ever-y youth cry wail a - way, Her name was Bar- b'ra Al - len. All in the mer - ry month of May, When green buds then were swell - ing, Young Ja - mie Grove on his death-bed lay For love of Bar- b'ra Al - len.

1. In Scarlet Town where I was born,
   There was a fair maid dwelling,
   Made every youth cry wail away,
   Her name was Barbara Allen.
   All in the merry month of May,
   When green buds then were swelling,
   Young Jamie Grove on his deathbed lay
   For love of Barbara Allen.

2. And death is printed on his face,
   And o'er his heart is stealin';
   Then haste away to comfort him,
   O lovely Barbara Allen.

So slowly, slowly she came up,
 And slowly she came nigh him:
And all she said when there she came,
 "Young man, I think you're dying."

3. He turned his face unto the wall,
 And death was with him dealin'.
"Adieu, adieu, my friends all,
 Adieu Barbara Allen!"
As she was walkin' o'er the fields,
 She heard the bells a-knellin';
And every stroke did seem to say
 "Unworthy Barbara Allen."

4. She turned her body round about,
 She spied the corpse a-coming;
"Lay down, lay down the corpse," she said,
 "That I may look upon him."
With scornful eyes she looked down,
 Her cheeks with laughter swelling,
Whilst all her friends cried out amain,
 "Unworthy Barbara Allen."

5. When he was dead and in his grave,
 Her heart was struck with sorrow;
"Oh, mother, mother, make my bed
 For I shall die tomorrow.
Hardhearted creature him to slight,
 Who loved me so dearly,
Oh that I'd been more kind to him,
 When he was alive and near me."

6. She on her deathbed as she lay,
 Begged to be buried by him,
And sore repented of the day
 That she did ere deny him.
"Farewell," she said, "ye maidens all
And shun the fault I fell in.
Henceforth take warning by the fall
 Of cruel Barbara Allen."

*B*

"Barbara Allen." Communicated by Miss Martha M. Davis, of the Win-
throp College faculty, Rock Hill, S. C. She obtained it from one of her students,
Miss Elizabeth Sharp, of Leslie, S. C., in whose family both text and tune
are traditional.

It was up-on a high high hill Two maidens chose their dwelling. And

one was known both far and wide Was known as Bar-b'ra Al-len.

1.  It was upon a high, high hill
       Two maidens chose their dwelling;
    And one was known both far and wide,
       Was known as Barbara Allen.

2.  'Twas in the merry month of May,
       All the flowers blooming,
    A young man on his death bed lay
       For the love of Barbara Allen.

3.  He sent a servant unto her
       In the town where she was dwelling.
    "Come, Miss, O Miss, to my master dying
       If your name be Barbara Allen."

4.  Slowly, slowly she got up,
       And to his bedside going,
    She drew the curtain to one side,
       And said, "Young man you're dying."

5.  He stretched one pale hand to her
       As though he would to touch her.
    She hopped and skipped across the floor.
       "Young man," says, "I won't have you.

6. "Remember, 'member in the town,
    'T was in the tavern drinking,
   You drank a health to the ladies all
    But you slighted Barbara Allen."

7. He turned his face toward the wall,
    His back upon his darling.
   "I know I shall see you no more,
    So goodbye, Barbara Allen."

8. As she was going to her home,
    She heard the church bell tolling.
   She looked to the east and looked to the west,
    And saw the corpse a-coming.

9. "O hand me down that corpse of clay
    That I may look upon it.
   I might have saved that young man's life,
    If I had done my duty.

10. "O Mother, Mother, make my bed;
     O make it long and narrow.
    Sweet William died for me today,
     I shall die for him tomorrow."

11. Sweet William died on a Saturday night,
     And Barbara Allen on a Sunday.
    The old lady died for the love of them both,
     She died on Easter morning.

12. Sweet William was buried in one graveyard,
     Barbara Allen in another;
    A rose grew on Sweet William's grave
     And a brier on Barbara Allen's.

13. They grew and they grew to the steeple top,
     And there they grew no higher;
    And there they tied in a truelover knot,
     The rose clung round the brier.

## C

"Barbara Allen." Communicated by Professor H. A. Wise, of Converse College, Spartanburg, S. C., in 1913. Professor Wise recorded it in a Richland County mill village.

1. Yonder come three maids,
   All dressed in scarlet red,
   And there is not but one that I call mine,
   And that is Barbara Allen,
   And that is Barbara Allen.
   There is not but one that I call mine,
   And that is Barbara Allen.

2. It was in the fall time of the year,
   When cider was a-broaching,
   He handed cider to the ladies round,
   But he slighted Barbara Allen.

3. Johnnie Green took very sick,
   He sent for Barbara Allen,
   He sent his servant to the town
   To search for Barbara Allen.

4. And slowly Barbara she got up,
   And slowly she came to him;
   She lifted the curtain where he lay,
   "Young man, I believe you are dying."

5. "I'm sick, I'm sick, I'm sick,
   I am in my death bed lying;
   And never will no better be
   Till I get Barbara Allen."

6. "You are sick, you are sick, you are very sick,
   You are on your death bed lying;
   And if you never no better be
   You will never get Barbara Allen.

7. "For it was in fall time of the year,
    When cider was a-broaching;
You handed cider to the ladies round,
    But you slighted Barbara Allen."

8. He turned his eyes upon the wall,
    Again he looked upon her;
"So fare you well to all my friends,
    But be kind to Barbara Allen."

9. She bade him good-bye and started home,
    With sorrow in her bosom;
She had not got far from the town
    When she heard strange bells a-ringing.

10. And she turned round and she looked back,
    And she saw his corpse a-coming:
"Unfold, unfold that milk white sheet,
    And let me look upon him."

11. The more she looked the more she wept,
    Until she grew far from him

    .   .    .    .    .

    .    .   .    .    .

12. "O Mother, O Mother, go make my bed!
    Go make it soft and easy;
For Johnnie Green died for me to-day,
    And I'll die for him to-morrow."

13. "O Father, O Father, go dig my grave,
    Go dig it deep and narrow;
For Johnnie Green died for me in love,
    I'll die for him in sorrow."

14. They dug two graves in Steven's yard,
    They dug them side by side;
In one they laid Johnnie Green,
    In the other Barbara Allen.

15. On Johnnie Green's there sprang a rose,
    On Barbara's sprang a brier;
They grew and grew to mountains high,
    For they could go no higher.
And there they tied in a true love knot
    For all young maids to admire.

## 𝒟

"Barbara Allen." Communicated from Darlington County, S. C., by a correspondent of *The State* newspaper, in which it appeared February 29, 1912, accompanied by the following account of its origin:

"It has been over forty years ago, when I was a boy at my father's home in Darlington County, my cousin sang the song as she frequently did, not only this one, but 'Sweet Alice, Ben Bolt,' 'Drummer Boy of Waterloo,' 'Kitty Wells,' 'When This Cruel War Is Over,' 'Who Will Care for Mother Now,' and others. I don't remember, if I ever knew, what were the troubles of Barbara Allen and Young William, but I remember the plaintive, mournful tune and it brings back to my recollection the scent of cape jessamine and mimosa blossoms, the note of the whippoorwill, and the peculiar halloo of the negroes."

The text is typical of most of the shorter South Carolina variants, as A is of the longer ones.

1. 'T was in the pleasant month of May,
    When all young buds were swelling;
Young William on his death bed lay
    For the love of Barbara Allen.

2. He sent his servant to her house,
    He sent him to her dwelling;
"My master's sick and sends for you
    If you be Barbara Allen."

3. She came at once unto his bed,
    And saw him gently lying;
She took one look at him and said,
    "Young man, I see you're dying.

4. "Oh! mother, mother, dig my grave,
    Dig it both deep and narrow;
Young William died for me today
    And I for him to morrow."

5. Young William died on Saturday morn,
   And Barbara died on Sunday,
And both the parents that Barbara loved,
   They died on Easter Monday.

## *E*

"Barbara Allen." Communicated, together with variant C, to the columns of *The State* newspaper, Feb. 29, 1912.

1. One Monday morning in the month of May,
   Sweet William courted a fair young girl,
Her name was Barbara Allen.
   He courted her six months or more, and was about to gain
      her favor,
When she says "O, wait, young man, do wait,
   For young men's minds do waver."

2. As he went home, was taken sick, and sent for Barbara Allen.
   She came; she came so slow, she came to see her true love
      dying.
She says: "Young man, you are a-dying."
   "One kiss from your red rosy lips would save me, Barbara
      Allen."
She says: "If one kiss would kill you dead, I'd freely give a
   hundred."

3. He turned his face to the milk-white walls; his back to Bar-
      bara Allen.
   "Don't you remember, the other day, when you were at
      the tavern,
You spent your wealth with the fair young girls, and slighted
   Barbara Allen?"
   "When I am dead, look under my head; you'll find two
      rolls of money.
Go share them around with the fair young girls, and share
   with Barbara Allen."

4. She had n't got more than a mile from town, when she heard
   the death bells ringing,
   She looked to the East and looked to the West, a-wringing
   her hands and crying.
   She looked up and down both ends of the road, and she saw
   his corpse a-coming.

5. She said: "Go bring him along, and let me look upon him.
   He once was red, but now he's dead — all his beauty has
   left him.
   Go dig my grave, dear Father," says she. "Go dig it long
   and deep,
   Sweet William died for me to-day, and I shall die to-
   morrow.
   Go make my pillow, Mother," says she. "Go make it long
   and narrow.
   Sweet William died for love to-day, and I shall die to-
   morrow."

6. Go bury Sweet William in one church yard, and Barbara in
   another.
   From Sweet William's grave there sprung a rose, from
   Barbara's sprung a briar.
   They grew to the new church wall, till they could grow no
   higher,
   There they wrapped and tied a true love's knot,
   That they might live and never part,
   And for all true-lovers to admire.

## F

"Bobree Allin," a negro variant, communicated in 1913.

1. In London town whar I were raised,
   Dar war a youth a-dwellin';
   He fell in love wid a pretty fair maid,
   Her name 't war Bobree Allin.

2. He co'ted her for seven long year,
   She said she would not marry.
   Poor Willie went home, and war taking sick,
   An ve'y likely died.

3. He sent out his waitin' boy
   Wid a note for Bobree Allin.
   So close-ah she read, so slow-ah she walked,
   "Go tell him I'm a-comin'."

4. She den step up into his room
   An' stood an' looked upon him.
   He stretched to her his pale white hands:
   "Oh, won't you tell me howdy?"

5. "Have you forgot de udder day,
   When we war in de pawlor;
   You drank your health to de gals aroun',
   And slighted Bobree Allin?"

6. "Oh no! oh no! my dear young miss;
   I think you is mistaking;
   Ef I drank my healt' to de gals aroun',
   'T was love for Bobree Allin.

7. "An' now I'm sick and ve'y sick,
   An' on my death-bed lyin';
   One kiss or two from you, my dear,
   Would take away dis dyin'."

8. "Dat kiss or two you will not git,
   Not if your heart was breakin';
   You dassent drink to de gals aroun'
   And slight Miss Bobree Allin."

9. He turn his pale face to de wall,
   An' den began er cryin';
   An every tear he shed appeared
   "Hard-a-hearted Bobree Allin."

10. She walked across de fiels nex' day,
    An' heard de birds a-singin';
    An' every note it seemed to say,
    "Hard-a-hearted Bobree Allin."

11. She war walkin' cross de fiel nex' day,
    An' spied his pale corpse comin';
    "Oh, lay him down upon de groun',
    An' let me look upon him."

12. As she war walkin down de street,
    She heerd de death-bells ringin';
    An' every tone dey seem to say,
    "Hard-a-hearted Bobree Allin."

13. "Oh, fader, fader, dig-ah my grave,
    An' dig it long an' narrow;
    My true love he have died today
    An' I must die tomorrow.

14. "Oh, mudder, mudder, make-ah my s'roud,
    An' make it long an narrow;
    Sweet Willie's died for de love of me,
    An' I mus' die tomorrow."

15. Sweet Willie war buried in de new church-yard,
    An' Bobree Allin beside him:
    Outen his grave sprang a putty red rose,
    And Bobree Allin's a brier.

16. Dey grew as high as de steeple top,
    An' could n't grow no higher;
    An' den dey tied a true love knot
    De sweet rose roun' de brier.

## G

"Barbara Allen." A variant of eleven stanzas, communicated by Mr. E. R. Aycock, of Clinton, S. C., in 1913.

## H

"Barbara Allen." Twelve stanzas communicated by Mrs. Emma Clement, of Spartanburg County, S. C., in 1913.

## I

"Barbara Allen." Seven stanzas, communicated by Mrs. P. N. Lott, of Johnston, S. C., in 1913.

## J

"Barbara Allen," Nine stanzas, communicated in 1914 by Professor C. Alphonso Smith, who secured it from a student at Knoxville, Tenn., Miss Claudia K. Townes, of Greenville, S. C. The tune is the same as *B* above.

## K

"Barbara Allen." Twelve stanzas, communicated by Professor H. C. Davis, of the University of South Carolina, in 1925. Professor Davis obtained it from one of his students, Mr. H. Cordle, who got it from Mrs. Howell, of Lexington County, S. C.

## L

"Barbara Allen." A variant from Greenville County, S. C.

## M

"Barbara Allen." A variant almost exactly like *A*, communicated by Miss Lillie Hall from Oconee County, S. C.

# IX

## LADY ALICE (GILES COLLINS)

### (CHILD, No. 85)

THE American title of this ballad is "Giles," "John," "George," or "Young Collins." Campbell and Sharp give five variants and five tunes, and Cox gives five texts. For other American variants and references, see Cox's head-note, p. 110. In plot, this ballad is the counterpart, or opposite, of "Lord Lovel," Child, No. 75.

"George Collins," communicated by Professor H. C. Davis, of the University of South Carolina, in 1925, who obtained it from H. Cordle, one of his students, who took it down from the singing of Mrs. Howell, of Lexington County, S. C. Mrs. Howell has been familiar with the ballad from childhood, and Mr. Cordle states that he has frequently heard it sung in the Dismal Swamp region of Virginia. Professor Davis says of the local version: "It is unquestionably one that has been orally transmitted, along with 'Barbara Allen,' in mill communities. This particular instance probably belongs in the stream of migration, of recent years, from the highlands of the state into the mill villages."

1. George Collins rode home last Wednesday night,
    He rode so slow and fine;
   George Collins rode home last Wednesday night,
    And there took sick and died.

2. His dearest Marrie was in yonder hall,
    A-sewing her silk so fine;
   So soon as she heard George Collins was dead,
    She laid it all aside.

3. She followed him up, she followed him down,
    She followed him to the ground;
   She fell upon bending knees,
    She cried, she wept, she moaned.

4. "O daughter, O daughter, don't grieve so hard,
    For there's more young men than George."
   "O mother, O mother, he is all my heart,
    And now I'm left alone.

5. "Don't you see yonder lonely dove,
    A-flying from pine to pine,
  A-weeping and a-mourning for his own true love;
    And why not me for mine?

6. "Sit down the coffin, lift up the lid,
    Spread back that sheet so fine,
  And let me kiss his cold clay lips;
    I am sure he will never kiss mine."

# X

# THE MAID FREED FROM THE GALLOWS

## (CHILD, No. 95)

CAMPBELL and Sharp give four texts and four tunes; Cox gives seven texts; Sharp gives one text with tune. For additional American references, see Cox's head-note, p. 115; and for English references, Sharp, Notes, pp. xxiv, xxv. The usual American title for this ballad is "The Hangman's Tree," or "The Ropeman." For an account of its extended career in oral tradition, see above pp. 80–94.

## *A*

"The Hangman's Tree." Communicated by Reed Smith, who heard the ballad in West Virginia in the summer of 1902. He was working with a surveyor's crew ten miles from the railroad in the mountains. One night, he heard one of the axemen singing a peculiar minor air. This man could neither read nor write and had lived in McDowell county all his life. As minors always have a strange fascination for amateur musicians, the young surveyor hummed the tune over several times till he learned it. It look no special effort to remember the words; they practically "learned themselves." Several years later, he found that this song, picked up so casually and accidentally in West Virginia, is an excellent American variant of "The Maid Freed from the Gallows."

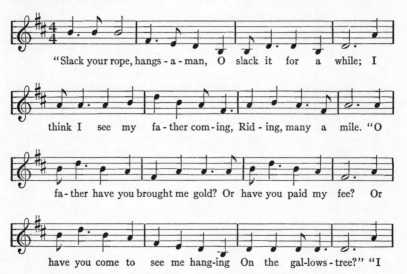

"Slack your rope, hangs - a - man, O slack it for a while; I think I see my fa - ther com - ing, Rid - ing, many a mile. "O fa - ther have you brought me gold? Or have you paid my fee? Or have you come to see me hang - ing On the gal - lows - tree?" "I

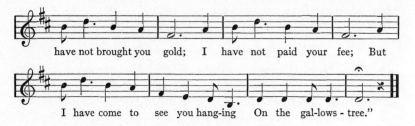

have not brought you gold; I have not paid your fee; But

I have come to see you hang-ing On the gal-lows - tree."

1. "Slack your rope, hangs-a-man,
    O slack it for a while;
    I think I see my father coming,
    Riding many a mile.

2. "O father have you brought me gold?
    Or have you paid my fee?
    Or have you come to see me hanging
    On the gallows-tree?"

3. "I have not brought you gold;
    I have not paid your fee;
    But I have come to see you hanging
    On the gallows-tree."

4. "Slack your rope, hangs-a-man,
    O slack it for a while;
    I think I see my mother coming,
    Riding many a mile.

5. "O mother have you brought me gold?
    Or have you paid my fee?
    Or have you come to see me hanging
    On the gallows-tree?"

6. "I have not brought you gold;
    I have not paid your fee;
    But I have come to see you hanging
    On the gallows-tree."

(And so on for brother, sister, aunt, uncle, cousin, etc.)

7. "Slack your rope, hangs-a-man,
    O slack it for a while;
I think I see my truelove coming
    Riding many a mile.

8. "O truelove have you brought me gold?
    Or have you paid my fee?
Or have you come to see me hanging
    On the gallows-tree?"

9. "Yes I have brought you gold;
    Yes, I have paid your fee;
Nor have I come to see you hanging
    On the gallows-tree."

### B

"The Scarlet Tree." Communicated by Mr. W. R. Dehon, of Summerville, S. C., in 1913. Mr. Dehon learned it from the singing of a colored nurse
many years ago. "The name of the nurse was Margaret," he writes. "She
belonged to my Uncle, the Rev. Paul Trapier, then rector of St. Michael's
Church, Charleston, who was living then, about 1856 or 1857, in my Great-
Grandfather's house, known as the 'N. R.' house, on Meeting Street next
south of the Scotch Church. It was when visiting at this house that we as
children used to hear Margaret recite 'The Hangman's Tree.'"

1. "Hangman, hangman, hold your hand
    A little longer still;
I think I see my father coming
    And he will set me free.

2. "Oh father, father, have you brought
    My golden ball and come to set me free?
Or have you come to see me hung
    Upon the Scarlet Tree?"

3. "I have not brought your golden ball,
    Or come to set you free;
But I have come to see you hung
    Upon the Scarlet Tree."

(So on through the family till the lover comes.)

"I have brought your golden ball;
    I come to set you free;
I have not come to see you hung
    Upon the Scarlet Tree."


## C

"The Hangman's Tree."   A variant from Richland County, S. C.


## D

"The Sorrow Tree."   A variant from Greenville County, S. C.


## E

"The Ropeman."   Communicated by Mrs. Iola Cooley King, of Williamston, S. C., in 1913.

# XI

## SIR HUGH, OR, THE JEW'S DAUGHTER

### (CHILD, No. 155)

CHILD gives twenty-one versions of this ballad, which agree rather closely in the outline of the story and in many of the details. In his version N, however, obtained in New York and recorded in Newell's *Games and Songs of American Children*, the boy's name has become Harry Hughes and the Jew's daughter is the Duke's daughter.

The story of the alleged murder of Hugh of Lincoln by Jews is told in the *Annals of Waverley*, under the year 1255, by a contemporary writer, and is also repeated and enlarged upon by Matthew Paris and in the *Annals of Burton*.

The oldest of the English ballads on this subject were recovered about the middle of the eighteenth century, and must have undergone many changes in the course of five hundred years of oral transmission.

The most famous literary form of the story is Chaucer's "Prioress's Tale." Compared with the ballad, it illustrates very significantly, as Professor Gummere points out,[1] the difference between "artless and artistic narrative."

Cox reports fourteen variants from West Virginia, six of which he gives in full. For other American occurrences see his detailed head-note, page 120.

"The Two Playmates," communicated by Mrs. E. L. Bolin, McCormick County, S. C., who as a child learned it from a playmate's grandmother in Spartanburg County.

FIRST STANZA

1. It rained, a-las! it rained, a-las! It sprinkled all o-ver the town. Two

lit - tle boys went out to toss a ball; To toss a ball.

SECOND STANZA

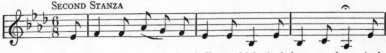

2. At first they tossed the ball too high; And then too low; And

---

[1] Gummere, p. 229. For a detailed comparison of the two, see Hart, Intro., pp. 30, 31.

then they tossed it in-to a yard Where no one was al-lowed to go.

STANZAS 4, 5, 6, 8, AND 9

4. "Oh, no! Oh, no!    I can't come in, Unless my playmate comes too; For

when lit-tle   boys come in your door They never come out any   more."

1. It rained, alas! it rained, alas!
       It sprinkled all over the town.
   Two little boys went out to toss a ball;
       To toss a ball.

2. At first they tossed the ball too high;
       And then too low;
   And then they tossed it into a yard
       Where no one was allowed to go.

3. A Jewish Lady came to the door,
       All dressed in silk so fine;
   "Come in, come in, my pretty little boys, come in."

4. "Oh, no! Oh, no! I can't come in,
       Unless my playmate comes too;
   For when little boys come in your door
       They never come out any more."

5. At first she showed him a bright red apple,
       And then a pretty red peach;
   And then she showed him a diamond ring,
       That called his little heart in.

6. And then she led him to the dining room,
       Where no one could hear his cry;
   And then she took a carving knife
       To carve his little heart in.

7. "Oh spare my life, oh spare my life,"
   The little boy cried.

   .   .   .   .   .   .   .   .
       .   .   .   .   .   .   .

8. "Well, place a Bible at my head,
   And a prayer book at my feet;
   And when my playmate calls for me,
   Pray tell him that I'm asleep.

9. "And place a prayer book at my feet,
   And a Bible at my head;
   And when my mother calls for me,
   Pray tell her that I am dead."

# XII

## JAMES HARRIS (THE DAEMON LOVER)

### (CHILD, No. 243)

CHILD gives eight versions of this interesting ballad. It was known in England and Scotland in the seventeenth century, and with the title "The Daemon Lover" was printed in Scott's *Ministrelsy of the Scottish Border*, fifth edition. Its usual title in America is "The House Carpenter," sometimes "The [House] Carpenter's Wife," or "The Salt Water Sea." Campbell and Sharp give eleven variants and tunes, and Cox twenty-one variants, five printed in full and the other sixteen described. For other American references, see Cox's head-note, p. 139.

Like most of the American survivals, our two versions lack the first part of the ballad story, which is as follows. The heroine plights her troth to a sailor, who is later forced to go to sea. After the usual three (or seven) years of waiting, she comes to the conclusion that her lover is dead, and marries a carpenter. Then the ghost or demon of her first lover (who has really perished) appears to her and claims her for his own. It is at this point that our texts begin, and they tell the rest of the story fully and consecutively enough. In the American survivals (as here) it does not appear that the returned lover is a ghost or demon. He figures merely as a flesh-and-blood lover. This is thoroughly in accord with the general principle that supernatural elements in the ballad gradually disappear as more recent times are reached. Compare, in this respect, modern survivals of "Lady Isabel and the Elf Knight," for example the South Carolina texts, pp. 97–100 above.

### A

"The House Carpenter." Communicated by Mrs. Emma Clement, of Spartanburg County, S. C., in 1913.

1. "Well met, well met, my old truelove
     Well met, well met, once more.
   I have just returned from my old native home
     And it's all for the sake of you.

2. "I could have married the king's daughter dear;
     I'm sure she would have married me;
   But I refused the crown of gold,
     And it's all for the sake of you."

3. "If you could have married the king's daughter dear,
    I'm sure you are to blame;
For I've just married a house carpenter,
    And I think he's a nice young man."

4. "If you will forsake your house carpenter,
    And go along with me,
I'll take you where the grass grows green
    On the banks of the cedar-see."

5. "If I do forsake my house carpenter,
    And go along with you;
What have you got to support me on
    And to keep me from slavery?"

6. "I have seven ships on the wide blue sea,
    All sailing for dry land,
One hundred and thirty-six sea jolly men,
    And they are all at your command."

7. They hadn't been gone more than two days,
    I'm sure it had not been three,
Till she began to weep and mourn
    And cry most pitifully.

8. "Are you a weeping for my gold?
    Or a weeping for my stores?
Or a weeping for your house carpenter,
    Whose face you'll see no more?"

9. "I'm neither weeping for your gold,
    Nor neither for your stores,
I'm weeping for my dear little babe,
    Whose face I'll see no more.

10. "Who will shoe its little feet?
    And who will glove its hands?
And who will kiss its rosy little lips
    When I'm so far from land?"

11. "Its father will shoe its little feet,
        And also glove its hands,
    And he will kiss its rosy little lips,
        When you're so far from land."

12. They had n't been gone more than three days,
        I'm sure, it had n't been four,
    Till there sprang a leak into the ship
        And it sank for to rise no more.

### ℬ

"The House Carpenter." Communicated by Mrs. Iola Cooley King, of
Williamston, S. C., in 1913.

1. "And it's we have met, and it's we have met,
        And it's we have met," says he.
    "I've just returned from the salt water sea;
        It was all for the love of thee,
        It was all for the love of thee.

2. "I could have married the king's daughter dear,
        She said she'd marry me;
    But I refused great crowns of gold;
        It was all for the love of thee,
        It was all for the love of thee."

3. "If you had married the king's daughter dear,
        I'm sure you had done wrong;
    For I have married the house carpenter,
        And I think him a neat little man,
        And I think him a neat little man."

4. "O won't you leave your house carpenter,
        And go along with me?
    I'll take you where the grass grows green
        On the banks of sweet re-lee."

5. "If I leave my house carpenter
        And go along with thee,
    O what have you got to maintain me on,
        And keep me from slavery?"

6. "I have seven fine ships on the shore,
    And seven more on the sea,
  And a hundred and ten of the jolly, jolly men,
    They are all for to wait on thee."

7. She called her babes all around her lap,
    The kisses one, two, three;
  "O stay with your papa dear,
    And keep him company
  Whilst I'm a-sailing on the sea."

8. She whirled herself all in her room,
    And she dressed herself in scarlet-green.
  She shone as bright as a morning star
    As she walked the streets alone.

9. She had not been on sea but one or two weeks,
    I'm sure it had not been three,
  Till this fair damsel gan to weep
    And she wept most bitterly.

10. "Are you weeping for my gold or my silver?
    Or 're you weeping for my store?
  Or 're you weeping for your house carpenter,
    The ones you'll never see no more?"

11. "I'm neither weeping for your gold or your silver,
    Nor either I'm a-weeping for your store;
  But I'm a-weeping for my sweet little babes,
    The ones I'll never see no more."

12. "Cheer up, cheer up, and go along with me,
    I'll take you where the grass grows green,
  On the banks of sweet re-lee,
    On the banks of sweet re-lee."

13. She had not been on sea but two or three weeks,
    I'm sure it had not been four;
    Till there sprang a leak in the bottom of the deck,
    And it sank for to rise no more.

14. "What an awful thing, what an awful thing,
    What an awful thing," says he;
    "Is for to steal of a house carpenter's wife,
    And now she's drownded in the sea."

# XIII

## ANDREW BARTIN

### (Henry Martyn)

### (Child, No. 250)

This ballad may have sprung from the longer and more stirring sea ballad of "Sir Andrew Barton," Child, No. 167. Child gives five versions, his E version being the one quoted here.

For references to American texts and recent English tradition, see *J.A.F.L.*, vol. xxx, p. 327.

"Andrew Bartin." Communicated by Miss Louise Porter Haskell as derived from General E. P. Alexander of South Carolina, and derived by him from the singing of a cadet at West Point Military Academy in the winter of 1856–57. Two or three slight corrections have been made by Mrs. A. C. Haskell, sister of General Alexander. This copy comes nearer than the others to the original "Andrew Bartin"; but stanzas 11–13 are derived from "Captain Ward," Child, No. 287, stanzas 8, 10.

Further slight corrections in the text printed here were made by Leonard L. Mackall in consultation with General E. P. Alexander, his great-uncle, after seeing Child's printed version. Mr. Mackall's letter to Professor G. L. Kittredge is dated South Island, Georgetown, S. C., Dec. 11, 1904. It also contains the first stanzas of the three following songs:

1. My name is Sam Hall, is Sam Hall.

2. Lord Lovell, he stood at his castle gate,
   A-combing his milk-white steed,
   Lady Nancy Belle came riding by,
   A-wishing her lover good speed.

3. A-walking one morning, one morning in spring,
   To hear the sweet birds and the nightingale sing,
   I saw a poor damsel a-walking alone
   Saying, "I'm a lorn maiden a far ways from home."

1. Three bold broth-ers of mer-rie Scotland, And three bold broth-ers were

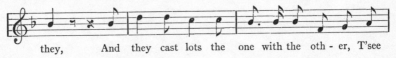

they, And they cast lots the one with the oth-er, T'see

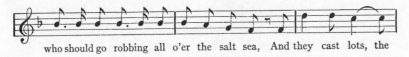

who should go robbing all o'er the salt sea, And they cast lots, the

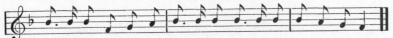

one with the oth - er, T'see who should go robbing all o'er the salt sea.

1. Three bold brothers of merrie Scotland,
   And three bold brothers were they,
   And they cast lots the one with the other,
   To see who should go robbing all o'er the salt sea;
   And they cast lots the one with the other,
   To see who should go robbing all o'er the salt sea.

2. The lot it fell on Andrew Bartin,
   The youngest of the three,
   That he should go robbing all o'er the salt sea,
   To maintain his two brothers and he.

3. He had not sailed but one long summer night,
   When daylight did appear;
   He saw a ship sailing far off and far round,
   At last she came sailing quite near.

4. "Who art?  Who art?" says Andrew Bartin,
   "Who art comes sailing so nigh?"
   "We are the rich merchants of merrie England,
   Just please for to let us pass by."

5. "Pass by? pass by?" says Andrew Bartin,
   "No, no, that never can be;
   Your ship and your cargo I will take away,
   And your brave men drown in the sea."

6. Now when this news reached merrie England —
   King George he wore the crown —
   That his ship and his cargo were taken away,
   And his brave men they were all drowned.

7. "Go build me a ship," says Captain Charles Stewart,
   "A ship both stout and sure,
And if I don't fetch this Andrew Bartin,
   My life shall no longer endure."

8. He had not sailed but one long summer night,
   When daylight did appear,
He saw a ship sailing far off and far round,
   At last she came sailing quite near.

9. "Who art? Who art?" says Captain Charles Stewart,
   "Who art comes sailing so nigh?"
"We are the bold robbers of merrie Scotland
   Just please for to let us pass by."

10. "Pass by? pass by?" says Captain Charles Stewart,
   "No, no, that never can be;
Your ship and your cargo I will take away,
   And your brave men carry with me."

11. "Come on! come on!" says Andrew Bartin,
   "I value you not one pin;
And though you are lined with good brass without,
   I'll show you I've fine steel within."

12. Then they drew up a full broadside
   And at each other let pour;
They had not fought for three hours or more,
   When Captain Charles Stewart gave o'er.

13. "Go home! go home!" says Andrew Bartin;
   "And tell your king from me,
That he may reign king of the merry dry land,
   But that I will be king of the sea."

# XIV

## OUR GOODMAN

### (CHILD, No. 274)

THIS rollicking bit of broad humor is a favorite in many lands. Child gives two versions. His A version (from Herd, 1776) swings on the following pivot of four stanzas and two recitatives:

Hame came our goodman,
    And hame came he,
And then he saw a saddle-horse
    Where nae horse should be.

"What's this now, good wife?
    What's this I see?
How came this horse here,
    Without the leave o' me?"

*Recitative:* "A horse?" quo she. "Ay, a horse," quo he.

"Shame fa your cuckold face,
    Ill mat ye see!
'T is naething but a broad sow,
    My minnie sent to me."

*Recitative:* "A broad sow?" quo he. "Ay, a sow," quo she.

"Far hae I ridden,
    And farer hae I gone,
But a sadle on a sow's back
    I never saw nane."

All the rest is incremental repetition on this frame. In the same way boots are explained as water-stoups (pitchers), a sword as a porridge-spurtle (stick for stirring), a wig as a clocken-hen (setting hen), a coat as a pair of blankets, and a man as a baby.

Child's B version has had an interesting career. It was translated into German in 1789 with a *dénouement* in which the man gives his wife a beating and explains his blows as caresses which her mother has sent her. This version, by the way, was taken over by the people and has had wide currency in oral tradition.

The ballad is still current both in Great Britain and in America, where it is usually called "Home came the old man." Cox gives three texts, and lists in his head-note, p. 154, other American references. Campbell and Sharp give three texts and three tunes.

"An Old Man Came Tumbling Home." Communicated by P. W. C.,
G. H. C., W. J. K., Jr., and R. S., of Columbia, S. C.

An old man came tumbling home, as drunk as he could be; He

found a horse with-in the stall Where his horse ought to be. "My

dear wife, my kind wife, My lov-ing wife," says he. "Whose

horse is that with-in the stall Where my horse ought to be?"

"You poor fool, you [blind] fool, You son of a [gun]," says she, "That's

noth-ing but a milk-cow Your moth-er gave to me." "I've

travelled the wide world o-ver, I've sailed from shore to shore; But a

sad-dle on a milk-cow I nev-er have seen be-fore."

I

An old man came tumbling home,
    As drunk as he could be;
He found a horse within the stall
    Where his horse ought to be.

"My dear wife, my kind wife,
    My loving wife," says he,
"Whose horse is that within the stall
    Where my horse ought to be?"

"You poor fool, you [blind] fool,
　You son of a [gun]," says she,
"That's nothing but a milk-cow
　Your mother gave to me."

"I've traveled the wide world over,
　I've sailed from shore to shore;
But a saddle on a milk-cow
　I never have seen before."


## 2

An old man came tumbling home,
　As drunk as he could be;
He found a hat upon the rack
　Where his hat ought to be.

"My dear wife, my kind wife,
　My loving wife," says he,
"Whose hat is that upon the rack
　Where my hat ought to be?"

"You poor fool, you [blind] fool,
　You son of a [gun]," says she,
"That's nothing but a peck-measure
　Your mother gave to me."

"I've traveled the wide world over,
　I've sailed from shore to shore;
But silk lining in a peck-measure
　I never have seen before."


(In the later stanzas a pair of pants is explained as a pumpkin-bag, a man's head as a baby, etc.)

# XV

## A PRETTY FAIR MISS

THIS song is traditional in Great Britain, where it is usually known as "The Sailor's Return." For British references, see Campbell and Sharp, p. 334.

It is likewise widely found in America, where the returned lover figures more often as a soldier than as a sailor. Variants have been recorded in Nova Scotia, Massachusetts, New York, Indiana, Kentucky, West Virginia, Virginia, North Carolina, South Carolina, and Georgia. For specific references, see Cox's head-note, p. 316. Cox gives two texts in full and mentions four others. Campbell and Sharp give five tunes and two full texts, under the title of "The Broken Token." This title comes from the old custom of lovers' breaking a token-ring and each keeping a half. This feature of the story does not occur in most American versions, but is found in one from West Virginia (Cox, A, st. 6, p. 317):

> He slipped his hand into his pocket,
>     His fingers being long and slim;
> He pulled the ring that was broken between them,
>     And at her truelove's feet she fell.

Most of the American tunes resemble each other unmistakably, and evidently come from the same original as the South Carolina tune given below. Two of the North Carolina tunes, however (Campbell and Sharp, B and E, pp. 282, 283), are decidedly minor, and differ not only from the others but from each other as well.

Mr. Carl Sandburg describes his variant in *The American Songbag* as "a whimsically sweet air going with an oddly spoken story," a description that applies also to the South Carolina variant.

"A Pretty Fair Miss." Communicated by Mrs. W. T. Adams, of Greenville, S. C., in 1927.

A pret-ty fair miss, all in a gar-den, A gay young man ... came rid-ing by; And as he rode, he so kind-ly ad-dressed her, "Oh say, fair miss, Won't you mar-ry me?"

1. A pretty fair miss, all in a garden,
    A gay young man came riding by;
   And as he rode, he so kindly addressed her,
    "Oh say, fair miss, won't you marry me?"

2. "Oh no, kind sir, a man of honor,
    A man of honor you may be;
   But how can you bear to propose to a lady
    Who is not fit for your bride to be?

3. I've got a sweetheart on the ocean.
    Seven long years been gone from me;
   But if he stays there seven years longer,
    No man on earth could a married me."

4. "Perhaps he's drownded on the ocean,
    Or in some fair battle slayed;
   Or if he's found him a fair lady married,
    And his fair face you'll see no more."

5. "If he's drownded I hope he's happy,
    Or in some fair battle slayed;
   Or if he's found him a fair lady married,
    I'll love the girl who married him."

6. He ran his hand all in his pocket,
    With his fingers slim and small;
   Saying, "Here's a gold ring you put on his finger."
    Straight down before him she did fall.

7. He picked her up all in his arms,
    Kisses gave her, one, two, three.
   Saying, "Seven long years I have been a sailor,
    Seven long years I have served my king.

8. "But if I'd stayed there seven years longer,
    No girl on earth could have married me."

(*In this variant, the song ends in the middle of the stanza,
giving a curious and plaintive effect.*)

# XVI

## HUNTING THE WREN OR "LET US GO TO THE WOODS"

Although this old nursery rhyme possesses slight value as either music or poetry, it has a long and interesting history. Its origins lie far back in the old English folk-custom of "hunting the wren" on St. Stephen's Day, December 26. Traces of the custom still linger here and there in Great Britain, and have been observed in Essex, Ireland, and the Isle of Man.

A detailed account of the St. Stephen's Day celebration in the Isle of Man is contained in G. F. Northall's *English Folk-Rhymes* (London, 1892), pp. 229–231, and is worth quoting from:

"In the Isle of Man the people account for the cruel persecution of the wren on this day (anciently, however, the custom was observed on December 24) by a tradition that formerly a siren used to bewitch numbers of the male population and lure them into the sea; and when at length a counter charm was employed to entrap her, she escaped by taking the form of a *wren*.

"But though she evaded instant annihilation, a spell was cast upon her by which she was condemned on every succeeding New Year's Day (*sic*), to reanimate the same form with the definite sentence that she must ultimately perish by human hand. Hence the persecution. It is believed that a single feather obtained from a wren killed on this day averts the danger of shipwreck. . . . When the chase ceases, one of the little victims is affixed to the top of a long pole with its wings extended, and carried in front of the hunters, who march in procession to every house, chanting:

'We hunted the wren for Robin the Bobbin,
We hunted the wren for Jack of the Can,
We hunted the wren for Robin the Bobbin,
We hunted the wren for every one.'

"After making the usual circuit and collecting all the money they could obtain, they laid the wren on a bier, and carried it in procession to the parish churchyard, where, with whimsical solemnity, they made a grave, buried it, and sang dirges over it in the Manx language, which they call her knell.

"At present there is not a particular day for pursuing the wren; it is captured by boys alone, who follow the old custom principally for amusement. On St. Stephen's Day a group of boys go from door to door with a wren suspended by the legs, in the centre of two hoops crossing each other at right angles, decorated with evergreens and ribbons, singing lines called *Hunt the Wren*. If at the close of this rhyme they are fortunate enough to obtain a small coin, they give in return a feather of the wren; and before the close of the day, the little bird may sometimes be seen hanging about featherless. The ceremony of the interment in the churchyard is now abandoned, and the seashore or some waste ground is substituted."

In *Gammer Gurton's Garland*, 1783, there is a version of seven stanzas entitled "Robin, Bobbin, Richard, and John, or The Wren Shooting." For other English references see W. Henderson, *Folklore of the Northern Counties*, 1879, p. 125, and T. F. T. Dyer, *British Popular Customs*, 1876, pp. 494–496.

Hall Caine, the novelist of Manx life, quotes the following stanza in his story, "Capt'n Davy's Honeymoon."

> "I'm hunting the wren," said Robbin to Bobbin,
> "I'm hunting the wren," said Richard to Robbin,
> "I'm hunting the wren," said Jack of the Lhen,
> "I'm hunting the wren," said every one.

Miss Louise Pound gives a Nebraska text in *American Ballads and Songs*, Charles Scribner's Sons, 1922, pp. 235, 236.

"Hunting the Wren." Communicated by Mrs. M. E. Thrower, of Cheraw, S. C., in 1924.

1. "Let us go to the woods," says Richard to Robin,
   "Let us go to the woods," says Robin to Bobbin,
   "Let us go to the woods," says John all alone,
   "Let us go to the woods," says everyone.

2. "What to do there?" says Richard to Robin,
   "What to do there?" says Robin to Bobbin,
   "What to do there?" says John all alone,
   "What to do there?" says everyone.

3. "We will shoot at a wren," says Richard to Robin, etc.

4. "How will we get her home?" etc.

5. "In a coach and six horses," etc.

6. "How will we dress her?" etc.

7. "We will hire seven cooks," etc.

8. "Then pounce! then pounce!" etc.

9. "She's dead! she's dead!" etc.

10. "We will have a great feast," etc.

# APPENDIX

# APPENDIX

## BALLADS SURVIVING IN AMERICA

IN tabulating American survivals of the traditional ballads, uniformity in terminology is desirable. As Professor Kittredge some years ago pointed out to the writer, both "ballad found in America" and "version" should be more strictly used. Ballad-collectors since Child include under "ballad found in America" all ballads secured from singers and reciters living in the United States, no matter what was the original nationality of singer or reciter. This is a proper use of the term if ballad-collectors unite in so using it, and if, furthermore, the same principle is followed in quoting statistics of American survivals listed in Child's published collection and in Child's ballad manuscripts.

Ballad-collectors usually employ "version" in the sense of "variant copy," and call each ballad copy or text a "version." In Child's collections, however, version means "a copy with distinguishing characteristics in plot, style, age, atmosphere, or the like," and a single version is often represented by several variants. Thus Child's Version B of Number 4 includes four variants (*a–d*), and his Version I of Number 12 includes nine variants (*a–i*).

A little more than ten years ago the writer undertook a ballad survey, with the idea of seeing just what ballads had been found in America.[1] Child's collection was examined for American survivals, Professor Kittredge kindly listed the American variants contained in the Child manuscripts in the Harvard University Library, and the results were combined with Mr. Barry's list printed by Professor H. M. Belden in his article on "Balladry in America."[2] With this as a basis, many of the leading ballad-

[1] See "The Traditional Ballad in the South," *J. A. F. L.*, vol. xxvii, and "The Traditional Ballad in the South During 1914," *Ibid.*, vol. xxviii.

[2] *Ibid.*, vol. xxv, p. 5, note 1.

collectors in the United States were consulted as to their individual collections, and all responded generously.[1] At that time (1915) the totals for the different Southern states were as follows: Tennessee, 8; Georgia, 9; Texas, 10; West Virginia, 12; South Carolina, 13; North Carolina, 19; Missouri, 20; Kentucky, 24; Virginia, 31. The total for the South was 42; for the United States, 76.

Gratifying progress has been made since then, and the last ten years have witnessed unusually rich ballad findings, particularly in North Carolina, West Virginia, and Virginia. The work of Mrs. Campbell and Mr. Sharp, as noted, resulted in the recovery of 37 traditional ballads, with 149 variants and tunes.

The valuable collection recently published [2] by Professor John Harrington Cox, of West Virginia, contains thirty-four traditional ballads with ten tunes. To his list Professor Josiah H. Combs's dissertation,[3] published the same year, adds five new ballads, making West Virginia's total 39. The Virginia collection has now reached the splendid total of 50 separate ballads, with 500 versions, variants, and fragments, and is soon to be printed.[4]

The fine North Carolina collection, which consists of 42 ballads in many versions and variants, may likewise be published in the near future.[5]

By combining these newer findings with the list made up in 1915, present totals may be derived as follows: In Campbell and Sharp there are eight ballads not hitherto reported in the South, — Nos. 3, 11, 54, 62, 99, 248, 272, 295, — four of which had not hitherto been reported in the United States — Nos. 54, 99, 248, 272. In Cox's collection there are four ballads new in

[1] Among these, in addition to Professor Kittredge and Mr. Barry, were Professor H. M. Belden of Missouri, Professor C. Alphonso Smith of Virginia, Professor Frank C. Brown of North Carolina, Professors J. A. Lomax and R. A. Law of Texas, and Miss Louise Pound of Nebraska.
[2] *Folk-Songs of the South*, Harvard University Press, 1925.
[3] *Folk-Songs du Midi des Etats-Unis*, University of Paris, 1925.
[4] Since the death of Professor C. Alphonso Smith, Professor Arthur Kyle Davis, Jr., of the University of Virginia, has assumed the work of editing the Virginia collection, and writes that it will be issued as soon as practicable.
[5] This material is in the hands of Professor Frank C. Brown, of Duke University, who was kind enough to list it for reference here.

the South, — Nos. 199, 214, 275, 283, — two of which were new in the United States — Nos. 199, 275. In the unpublished North Carolina and Virginia ballad material, listed through the kindness of Professor Brown and Professor Davis, respectively, there are eight ballads new in the South, — Nos. 1, 56, 65, 77, 114, 173, 221, 267, — five of which are new in the United States — Nos. 1, 56, 77, 114, 267.

Professor John R. Moore reported No. 218 from Southern Missouri in the *J. A. F. L.*, vol. xxxiv, pp. 395–397. In a personal letter to the writer, Jan. 22, 1927, Professor Cox reported No. 226 from West Virginia. Professor Combs, in *Folk-Songs du Midi des Etats-Unis*, lists five ballads from West Virginia new in the South: Nos. 43, 87, 100, 210, 240. Three of these, Nos. 87, 100, and 240, are likewise new for the United States.

Professor W. Roy Mackenzie has recorded in Nova Scotia a total of 15 ballads,[1] three of which have not been found in the United States, Nos. 88, 213, and 233.

So far as can be learned, that completes the list. The totals are: New England, 25; the South, 69; the United States, 92; Canada, 15; America, 95.

## BALLAD SURVIVALS IN THE UNITED STATES

N.B. Starred ballads are those *not* found in the South.

*Number in Child*

1. Riddles Wisely Expounded.
2. The Elfin Knight.
3. The Fause Knight Upon the Road.
4. Lady Isabel and the Elf-Knight.
7. Earl Brand.
10. The Twa Sisters.
11. The Cruel Brother.
12. Lord Randal.
13. Edward.
18. Sir Lionel.

---

[1] See his *The Quest of the Ballad*, Princeton University Press, 1919.

## Ballad Survivals in Canada

N. B. — Starred ballads are those *not* found in the United States.

F